Bernhard
Aichner

INNS'
BRUCK

Mit Texten von | *With texts by*
Georg Hasibeder

INNSB

Auflage | *Edition*:
4 3 2 1
2016 2015 2014 2013

HAYMON verlag
Innsbruck-Wien
www.haymonverlag.at

ISBN 978-3-7099-7070-6

Umschlag- und Buchgestaltung, Satz | *Cover and book design, typesetting*:
hœretzeder grafische gestaltung, Scheffau/Tirol

Fachliche Beratung: Lukas Morscher, Stadtarchiv/Stadtmuseum Innsbruck
Specialist advice: Lukas Morscher, City Archives/City Museum Innsbruck

Gedruckt auf umweltfreundlichem, chlor- & säurefrei gebleichtem Papier.
Printed on environmentally friendly, chlorine and acid free bleached paper.

Bernhard
Aichner

INNS'
BRUCK

BRUCK

Mit Texten von | *With texts by*
Georg Hasibeder

Fotografische Mitarbeit | *Photographic assistance:*
Bernhard Geiler

Innsbruck is a city with many faces: a tourist centre whose sights attract people from all over the world; a sporting and cultural city which hosts popular national events; a transport hub on the transit route between northern and southern Europe; and a gateway to the pristine mountains of the Alps. Above all, however, Innsbruck is home to over 120,000 townsfolk, who through their diversity shape the character of this city.

In this illustrated book we would like to invite you to discover the many facets of the Tyrolean capital. On the following pages you will find the well-known squares and buildings that should always be included in a portrait of Innsbruck. However, you will also come across views that are largely unknown even to those already familiar with the city and you will be able to re-examine many from an unusual perspective. This photographic journey through Innsbruck is thus intended not only to provide an encounter with its most beautiful aspects – but also to invite you to explore this unique city once again from the beginning.

Bernhard Aichner and Georg Hasibeder

FOREWORD | VORWORT

Innsbruck ist eine Stadt mit vielen Gesichtern: Tourismuszentrum, dessen Sehenswürdigkeiten Menschen aus aller Welt anlocken; Sport- und Kulturstadt mit Veranstaltungen von überregionaler Anziehungskraft; Verkehrsknotenpunkt an der Transitachse zwischen Nord- und Südeuropa; Eingangstor zur unberührten Bergwelt der Alpen. Vor allem aber ist Innsbruck die Heimat von über 120.000 Innsbruckerinnen und Innsbruckern, die in all ihrer Vielfalt den Charakter dieser Stadt prägen.

Mit diesem Bildband wollen wir Sie einladen, die zahlreichen Facetten der Tiroler Landeshauptstadt kennenzulernen. Auf den folgenden Seiten werden Sie bekannte Plätze und Bauwerke finden, die in einem Porträt von Innsbruck nicht fehlen dürfen. Ebenso treffen Sie auf Ansichten, die auch Kennern dieser Stadt weitgehend unbekannt sind, und werden vieles aus ungewohnten Blickwinkeln neu betrachten können. So soll dieser fotografische Streifzug durch Innsbruck nicht nur eine Begegnung mit seinen schönsten Seiten sein – sondern auch eine Einladung, diese einzigartige Stadt immer wieder von Neuem zu entdecken.

Bernhard Aichner und Georg Hasibeder

Stadt zwischen den Bergen

Als „Hauptstadt der Alpen" wird Innsbruck häufig bezeichnet, ein Titel, den die Stadt ganz zu Recht trägt: Innsbruck liegt nicht nur auf der Landkarte mitten im Alpenbogen, der sich von Südfrankreich bis kurz vor Wien zieht. Die unmittelbare Nachbarschaft zur alpinen Bergwelt macht auch den einzigartigen Charakter der Stadt aus: Hier die steil aufragende Nordkette, dort die bewaldeten Flanken des Patscherkofels, und dazwischen füllen die Häuser von Innsbruck den Talboden des Inntals.

Die Beziehung zwischen Stadt und Gebirge ist nicht frei von Spannungen. Die Berghänge setzen dem Wachstumsdrang der Stadt eine natürliche Grenze und machen bebaubare Flächen zu einem raren und teuren Gut. Darüber hinaus bedeuten die alpinen Naturgewalten mit Wildbächen, Muren und Lawinen auch eine stete Bedrohung vor allem für die Stadtteile am Fuß der Nordkette.

Andererseits ist die Nachbarschaft zum Gebirge auch ein „Markenzeichen" und das größte Kapital für Innsbruck als Sport- und Tourismusstadt: Knapp fünf Millionen Gäste besuchen Innsbruck pro Jahr und tragen – bei allen Problemen, die der moderne Tourismus auch mit sich bringt – wesentlich zum Wohlstand der Stadt bei.

Und nicht zuletzt sind die Berge rund um Innsbruck das liebste Naherholungsgebiet der Einheimischen. Sie finden hier ein reichhaltiges Angebot an Seilbahnen, Wanderwegen und Almhütten, Sportmöglichkeiten für jeden Geschmack und jede Jahreszeit: Mountainbikerouten, Klettergärten und -steige, Langlaufloipen, Rodelbahnen und Skipisten – und das alles in unmittelbarer Stadtnähe. Nicht einmal eine halbe Stunde dauert es, um von der Innenstadt mit öffentlichen Verkehrsmitteln auf die Nordkette zu gelangen.

Und wem der Sinn nach noch mehr Abgeschiedenheit steht, findet auch das in Innsbruck: am höchsten Punkt des Stadtgebiets etwa, der 2.642 m hohen Westlichen Praxmarerkarspitze, mehr als 2.000 m über dem Niveau des Inntals. Gute sieben Stunden braucht man von der Seilbahnstation am Hafelekar bis zu diesem Gipfel, der sich weit hinter der Nordkette versteckt. Während das Stadtgebiet im Süden nämlich nicht einmal bis zur Bergstation der Patscherkofel-Seilbahn reicht, umschließt es im Norden große Teile des Karwendelgebirges. Insgesamt bedecken Gebirgsflächen, Almen und Wälder mehr als 70 % des Gemeindegebiets von Innsbruck, nicht einmal 15 % der Fläche sind bebaut.

Wer von Innsbruck spricht, spricht also von beidem: von der lebhaften Stadt ebenso wie vom Gebirge rundum, von der urbanen Kultur wie von der Natur – eine Ambivalenz, die Innsbruck seit seiner Gründung prägt und die der Stadt bis heute ihren unverwechselbaren Charme verleiht. ■

City between the mountains

Innsbruck is commonly referred to as the "Capital of the Alps", a title that the city quite rightly bears. It's not only on the map that Innsbruck is located at the centre of the Alpine Arc, which stretches from the South of France to just before Vienna. The immediate vicinity to the Alps also accounts for the unique character of the city: on the one side the towering Nordkette, on the other side the forested flanks of the Patscherkofel, and down below, in between them, the houses of Innsbruck cover the floor of the Inn Valley.

The relationship between city and mountains is not free of tension. The mountain slopes create a natural limit to the growth of the city and transform any buildable plots of land into a rare and expensive commodity. In addition, natural hazards like torrents, landslides and avalanches represent a constant threat, especially to the districts at the foot of the Nordkette.

On the other hand, the proximity of the mountains is also a "trademark" and the largest asset for Innsbruck as a city of sports and tourism. Nearly five million people visit Innsbruck each year and despite all the problems that modern tourism brings – they contribute significantly to the prosperity of the city.

And last but not least, the mountains around Innsbruck form the favourite recreational area for locals. There is a wide range of cable cars, hiking trails and mountain huts – sporting opportunities for every taste and every season:

Mountain bike trails, climbing parks and climbing trails, cross-country skiing, sledding and ski slopes – all in the immediate vicinity of the city. It takes less than half an hour to get from the city centre to the Nordkette by public transport.

And anyone seeking even more seclusion can also find this in Innsbruck: for instance at the highest point of the urban area, the 2,642 m high Western Praxmarerkarspitze, which is more than 2,000 m above the level of the Inn Valley. It takes a good seven hours from the cable car station at the Hafelekar up to this summit which is hidden behind the Nordkette. While the urban area in the south does not even extend to the mountain station of the Patscherkofel cable car, it includes large parts of the Karwendel Mountains in the north. In total, mountainous areas, pastures and forests cover more than 70 % of the municipal territory of Innsbruck. Less than 15 % of the area has been built up.

When one thinks of Innsbruck, one therefore thinks of both the bustling city as well as the surrounding mountains, the urban culture as well as nature – an ambivalence that has characterised Innsbruck ever since its foundation and today lends the city its distinctive charm. ■

Unter der Felsmauer der Nordkette, zwischen dem Vorderen Brandjoch (links) und der Rumer Spitze (rechts), breitet sich die Stadt aus.

The town is spread out under the rocky wall of the Nordkette, between the Vorderes Brandjoch (left) and the Rumer Peak (right).

Im Norden wie im Süden bilden Berge die Grenze des Innsbrucker Siedlungsraums: das Karwendel mit der Nordkette (oben) und die Tuxer Alpen mit dem Patscherkofel (unten).

In the north as in the south, mountains form the boundary of the populated area of Innsbruck: the Karwendel with the Nordkette (above) and the Tux Alps with the Patscherkofel (below).

Die Hafelekarspitze ist der am leichtesten erreichbare Gipfel Innsbrucks: In wenigen Minuten leitet ein Weg von der Bergstation der Nordkettenbahn zum großen Gipfelkreuz.

The Hafelekars peak is the most accessible summit from Innsbruck. It takes just a few minutes along a path from the mountain station of the Nordkettenbahn to the large summit cross.

GIPFEL DER KONTRASTE Wie nahe Stadt und Gebirge, Wildnis und Zivilisation in Innsbruck beisammenliegen, wird nirgends so deutlich wie hier auf der Nordkette. Blickt man nach Süden, liegt einem die Stadt zu Füßen; auf ihrer Rückseite aber erstreckt sich eine alpine Urlandschaft aus Schotter und Fels. Dazwischen befindet sich auf der Seegrube das Bergsportzentrum Innsbrucks: Skipisten und Snowboarderpark im Winter, Wanderwege, Mountainbike-Singletrail und Klettersteig im Sommer, und all das nur wenige Seilbahnminuten von der Stadt entfernt.

SUMMIT OF CONTRASTS *The proximity of Innsbruck to both city and mountains, wilderness and civilisation, is nowhere more apparent than here on the Nordkette. If you look to the south, the city lies at your feet. However an alpine primeval landscape of gravel and rock stretches out just behind the city. In between on the Seegrube is the mountain sports centre of Innsbruck: skiing and snowboarding park in winter, hiking trails, mountain bike trails and climbing in the summer, and all just a few minutes away from the city by cable car.*

Die Gondel der neuen Hafelekar-Bahn von 2007 fährt in die 1928 nach Plänen von Franz Baumann, einem Pionier der alpinen Architektur, erbaute Bergstation ein.

Since 2007, the cable car of the new Hafelekar-Bahn has been operating at the mountain station which was built in 1928 according to plans by Franz Baumann, a pioneer of alpine architecture.

In einer halben Stunde vom Stadtzentrum ins Hochgebirge: Die Nordkettenbahn unterhalb der Seegrube.

From the city centre to the lofty mountains in half an hour: The cable car of the Nordkettenbahn below the Seegrube.

Hinter der Rumer Spitze liegt die Pfeishütte, Ausgangspunkt für anspruchsvolle Bergtouren im Karwendel.

Behind the Rumer Peak is the Pfeishütte, the starting point for demanding mountain tours in the Karwendel.

AUF DER HÖTTINGER ALM ... Glaubt man der Sage, so lebt auf der Höttinger Alm – ebenso wie einst auf der Umbrüggler Alm – ein Kasermandl: Ein uraltes, verhutzeltes Mandl, das als Strafe für sein frevelhaftes Tun – es soll mit Butterkugeln gekegelt haben – als Geist auf der Alm hausen muss. Das Kasermandl ist ein unberechenbarer Geselle, es kann freundlich sein, aber auch bösartig und gehässig. Will man es erlösen, so muss man dessen selbstgekochtes „Muas" essen – in das neben Mehl und Milch auch Dreck und Tierkot gemischt ist.

ON THE HÖTTINGER ALM ... *If you believe the legend, a "Kasermandl" lives on the Höttinger Alm – just as once on the Umbrüggler Alm. An ancient wizened fellow who as punishment for his outrageous actions – he is supposed to have bowled with butter balls – must dwell as a spirit on the mountain. The Kasermandl is an unpredictable fellow who can be friendly but also vicious and spiteful. If you wish to liberate him from his fate, you have to eat a home-cooked "Muas" – into which, in addition to flour and milk, dirt and animal dung are also mixed.*

Die Höttinger Alm ist ein beliebtes Ziel von Mountainbikern und Wanderern.

The Höttinger Alm is a popular destination for mountain bikers and hikers.

Bis heute werden die Almen rund um Innsbruck von Schafen und Kühen beweidet.

Even today the mountain pastures around Innsbruck are grazed by sheep and cows.

Aussichtsreich liegt die Bodensteinalm hoch über der Stadt.

The Bodensteinalm overlooks the city majestically.

Die Morgensonne, noch hinter dem Bettelwurf verborgen, taucht den Himmel in oranges Licht.

The morning sun, still hidden behind the Bettelwurf, bathes the sky in orange light.

Der Betonviadukt erinnert an die alte Hungerburgbahn, die von 1906 bis 2005 die Innenstadt mit „Hoch-Innsbruck" verband.

The concrete viaduct is reminiscent of the old Hungerburg funicular that connected the inner city with "Hoch-Innsbruck" [Upper Innsbruck] from 1906 to 2005.

DABEI SEIN IST ALLES Die Olympischen Winterspiele 1964 und 1976 waren einschneidende Ereignisse in der jüngeren Geschichte Innsbrucks: TV-Sender trugen die Bilder von Innsbruck in alle Länder und machten die Stadt als attraktives Zentrum des Wintersports weltweit bekannt. Auch im Stadtbild haben die Winterspiele dauerhafte Spuren hinterlassen: nicht nur mit Sportanlagen wie dem Eisstadion oder dem Eiskanal in Igls, wo neben Bob- und Rodelwettbewerben auch die Herrenabfahrt am Patscherkofel ausgetragen wurde. Auch das Olympische Dorf, wo sich die Athletenwohnheime befanden, erinnert an die olympische Ära Innsbrucks.

BEING THERE IS EVERYTHING *The Winter Olympics in 1964 and 1976 were significant events in the recent history of Innsbruck. TV stations carried the images of Innsbruck all over the world and made the city known worldwide as an attractive centre for winter sports. The Winter Games have also left lasting traces on the cityscape. Not only through sports facilities such as the ice arena or ice track in Igls where, in addition to bob sled and luge competitions, the men's downhill took place on the Patscherkofel. Also the Olympic Village, site of the athletes' residences, reminds one of Innsbruck's Olympic era.*

Der markante Sendeturm krönt den Gipfel des Patscherkofels.

The prominent radio tower crowns the summit of the Patscherkofel.

Seit 1929 führt eine Seilbahn von Igls auf den Patscherkofel.

Since 1929 a cable car crosses the distance from Igls to the Patscherkofel.

Unterhalb des Patscherkofels liegen die Stadtteile Igls und Vill auf einer weitläufigen Mittelgebirgsterrasse.

Below the Patscherkofel the districts Igls and Vill lie on a vast low mountain range.

BÄR, GEIER UND ADLER 1962 gründete der Zoologe Hans Psenner den Innsbrucker Alpenzoo mit drei Gehegen für Braunbär, Bartgeier und Steinadler. Gut 50 Jahre später beherbergt der höchstgelegene Zoo Europas 2.000 Tiere aus ca. 150 verschiedenen Arten, die in den Alpen heimisch sind oder – wie der Elch – waren. Unbestrittene Könige des Alpenzoos sind die Bärendame Martina und ihr junger Freund, den die Tiroler in Anlehnung an Andreas Hofer auf den Namen Ander getauft haben.

BEARS, VULTURES AND EAGLES *In 1962, the zoologist Hans Psenner founded the Innsbruck Alpine Zoo with three enclosures for: brown bears, bearded vultures and golden eagles. Some 50 years later, the highest zoo in Europe now houses 2,000 animals of around 150 different species that are native to the Alps – or used to be as in the case of the moose. Undisputed royalty of the Alpine Zoo are the female bear Martina and her young male friend, who was christened Ander in deference to the Tyrolean fondness for Andreas Hofer.*

Über 7.000 Pflanzenarten aus aller Welt – vom Mammutbaum bis zu heimischen Kräutern – zeigt der Botanische Garten der Universität Innsbruck (unten). In seiner Außenstelle, dem Alpengarten Patscherkofel (rechts), kann man die alpine Pflanzenwelt inmitten der Natur erwandern.

Over 7,000 plant species from around the world, from the Redwood Tree to local herbs, are displayed at the Botanical Garden of the University of Innsbruck (below). In one of its branches, the Patscherkofel Alpine Garden (right), one can discover the flora of the Alps in its natural environment.

Eine der grünen Oasen Innsbrucks ist der Rapoldipark in Pradl, benannt nach dem sozialdemokratischen Vizebürgermeister Martin Rapoldi (1880–1926).

One of the green oases in Innsbruck is the Rapoldipark in Pradl, named after the Social Democratic Deputy Mayor Martin Rapoldi (1880–1926).

Der Innsbrucker Hofgarten wandelte sich in den vergangenen 600 Jahren von einem höfischen Jagdrevier zur prächtigen Barockanlage und später zum Park im Englischen Stil, der bis heute die „grüne Lunge“ der Innsbrucker Innenstadt bildet.

Over the past 600 years the Innsbruck Hofgarten [Court Garden] has transformed from courtly hunting grounds to a magnificent baroque garden and later to an English-style park, which still forms the "green lung" of Innsbruck's city centre today.

LEBENSADERN UND GEFAHRENQUELLEN Über Jahrhunderte hinweg dienten die Flüsse und Bäche Innsbrucks als Verkehrswege und als Grundlage für die Wirtschaft – der Mühlauer Bach etwa trieb zahlreiche Mühlen und Sägewerke an. Und bis heute versorgen die Quellen an den Berghängen die Stadt mit Trinkwasser von einzigartiger Qualität. Gleichzeitig jedoch bedeutet das Wasser auch eine Bedrohung für die Stadt: Wildbäche zu beiden Seiten des Inntals sorgten immer wieder für Vermurungen und Überflutungen ganzer Stadtteile – eine Gefahr, die erst in den vergangenen Jahrzehnten durch Verbauungsmaßnahmen gebannt werden konnte.

LIFELINES AND HAZARDS *For centuries the rivers and streams of Innsbruck have served as transit routes and as a foundation for business – for instance the Mühlauer Bach [Mühlauer stream] operated numerous mills and sawmills. And to this day the sources on the mountain slopes supply the city with drinking water of exceptional quality. However the water also represents a threat to the city. Streams on both sides of the Inn valley have repeatedly caused mudslides and flooding of entire neighbourhoods – a danger which could only be dispelled in recent decades through extensive river engineering.*

Kurz bevor die Sill in den Inn einmündet, durchfließt sie die Sillschlucht am Fuß des Bergisels.

Shortly before the Sill joins the Inn, it flows through the Sill gorge at the foot of the Bergisel.

Der Baggersee in der Rossau ist der größte (Bade-)See Innsbrucks.

The quarry pond in the Rossau is the largest (swimming) lake in Innsbruck.

Der Hans-Psenner-Steg, der den Inn im Stadtteil Saggen überbrückt, ist nach dem Gründer des Alpenzoos benannt.

The Hans-Psenner-Steg, which spans the Inn in the Saggen, is named after the founder of the Alpine Zoo.

Der Spanische Saal auf Schloss Ambras, von Ferdinand II. als repräsentativer Festsaal errichtet, wird heute auch als Konzertsaal genutzt.

The Spanish Hall at Ambras Castle, built by Ferdinand II as a prestigious banquet hall, is now used as a concert hall.

Prunkvolle Zeichen der Macht

Im Jahr 1420 erhob Herzog Friedrich IV. – der seinem Spottnamen „Friedl mit der leeren Tasche" zum Trotz 1439 als reicher Mann starb – Innsbruck zur Residenzstadt und läutete damit eine erste Blütezeit der Stadt ein. Seine Residenz errichtete Friedrich im Neuhof am Stadtplatz – in jenem Gebäude, dessen Erker Kaiser Maximilian rund 80 Jahre später als „Goldenes Dachl" mit 2.657 vergoldeten Kupferschindeln decken ließ.

Hatte Friedrichs Residenz noch das Aussehen eines gewöhnlichen Bürgeransitzes, so ließ sein Sohn Erzherzog Sigmund – der seinem Beinamen „der Münzreiche" zum Trotz 1496 verarmt starb – die erste Hofburg am Rand der Altstadt erbauen. Sie sollte nicht nur würdiges Zentrum der Landesherrschaft sein, sondern auch sichtbares Zeichen von deren Macht und Größe.

Ihr heutiges Erscheinungsbild gab der Hofburg im 18. Jahrhundert Kaiserin Maria Theresia, die sie zum „Klein Schönbrunn der Alpen" umgestalten ließ: ein Gesamtkunstwerk, das die Handschrift von Johann Martin Gumpp d. J. zeigt. Er war ein Spross der großen Künstlerfamilie Gumpp, die über 200 Jahre hinweg ihre Spuren im Stadtbild von Innsbruck hinterlassen hat.

Prachtbauten als Stein gewordene Insignien der Macht – diese Idee erlebte ihren Höhepunkt unter Kaiser Maximilian I. Er schuf nicht nur mit dem Goldenen Dachl ein Bauwerk, das jedem Besucher der Stadt den Reichtum ihres Herrschers vor Augen führte. In der „Schwarzmanderkirche" genannten Hofkirche ließ er sich ein Denkmal errichten, das sein „gedechtnus" für alle Zeit bewahren sollte: 28 überlebensgroße Bronzefiguren bewachen das größte (wenn auch leere) Kaisergrab des Abendlandes, auf dem – hoch über allen anderen – der bronzene Maximilian kniet.

Maximilians Urenkel Erzherzog Ferdinand II. schenkte Innsbruck sein wohl prächtigstes Bauwerk: Er ließ Schloss Ambras im 16. Jahrhundert zu einem der schönsten Renaissanceschlösser Europas umgestalten. Ferdinand, der Ambras zudem seine berühmte Kunstsammlung hinterließ, übergab das Schloss seiner bürgerlichen Ehefrau Philippine Welser, die er heimlich und gegen den Willen seines Vaters geheiratet hatte. Sie sollte hier, abseits der städtischen Hofburg, eine würdige Residenz erhalten.

Mit dem Tod des Landesfürsten Sigismund Franz 1665 endete zwar Innsbrucks Ära als Residenzstadt, doch weiterhin besaß die Stadt hohen Stellenwert für den Hof: Kaiserin Maria Theresia verbrachte mit ihrer Familie viele Monate in Innsbruck, so zum Beispiel 1765 rund um die Hochzeit ihres Sohnes Erzherzog Leopold, an die heute noch die Triumphpforte erinnert – neben den Schlössern und Adelssitzen Innsbrucks bewahrt auch sie den Prunk und Reichtum früherer Zeiten bis in die Gegenwart. ■

Magnificent symbols of power

In 1420, Duke Friedrich IV – who, in spite of his nickname "Friedrich of the Empty Pockets", died a rich man in 1439 – honoured the city of Innsbruck by designating it as his city of residence and thus heralded its first period of prosperity. Friedrich made the Neuhof in the town square his residence – the building which around 80 years later had its oriel covered with 2,657 gilded copper tiles by Emperor Maximilian.

In contrast to Friedrich's residence which still endeavoured to maintain the appearance of an ordinary bourgeois property, his son Archduke Sigmund – who, in spite of his nickname "the Rich", died impoverished in 1496 – built the first Imperial Palace on the edge of the Old Town. It was intended not only to serve as a worthy centre for the state rulers, but also as a visible symbol of their power and greatness.

In the 18th century Empress Maria Theresa provided the Imperial Palace with its modern day appearance, converting it into the "Little Schönbrunn of the Alps": a total work of art that bears the hallmark of Johann Martin Gumpp Jr. He was a scion of the great Gumpp artist clan, who left their mark on the cityscape of Innsbruck for over 200 years.

Magnificent buildings of stone transformed into symbols of power – this idea reached its zenith under Emperor Maximilian I. Not only did he build the Golden Roof to impress every visitor to the city with the wealth of its ruler, but in the Court Church, known as the "Schwarzmanderkirche", he constructed a monument which was to preserve his memory for all time. Twenty-eight larger than life bronze statues guard the biggest (albeit empty) tomb of an emperor in the Western World. On top of it – high above all others – the bronze Maximilian kneels.

Maximilian's great-grandson Archduke Ferdinand II presented Innsbruck with arguably its most magnificent building. In the 16th century he had the Ambras Castle remodelled into one of the most beautiful Renaissance castles in Europe. Ferdinand, who furthermore left his famous art collection to Ambras, gave the castle to his bourgeois wife Philippine Welser, whom he had married secretly and against his father's wishes. Here, she was to obtain a worthy residence, far away from the Imperial Palace.

Although the death of Prince Sigismund Franz in 1665 ended Innsbruck's era as a seat of royal power, the city still retained great importance for the Court. Empress Maria Theresa and her family spent many months in Innsbruck, for example in 1765 around the time of the wedding of her son, Archduke Leopold. The event was commemorated by constructing a Triumphal Arch, which in addition to the castles and noble residences in Innsbruck preserves the splendour and wealth of earlier times for the present. ■

Die Innsbrucker Hofburg erhielt ihre heutige Gestalt im Stil des Wiener Rokoko unter Kaiserin Maria Theresia.

The Innsbruck Imperial Palace acquired its current form in the style of Viennese Rococo under Empress Maria Theresa.

Die Innenräume der Hofburg – der „Riesensaal" (links) oder das Toilettezimmer (unten) – vermitteln einen Eindruck vom höfischen Prunk früherer Tage.

The interiors of the Imperial Palace, the "Riesensaal" [Hall of Giants] (left) and the cloakrooms (below), convey an impression of the courtly splendour of former days.

Der Rennweg vor der Hauptfassade der Hofburg erinnert an die Turniere und Pferderennen, die hier bereits zur Zeit Maximilians I. stattgefunden haben.

The Rennweg in front of the main façade of the Imperial Palace is reminiscent of the tournaments and horse races that already took place here at the time of Maximilian I.

DENKMAL EINES ABWESENDEN Demütig kniet der in Bronze gegossene Kaiser Maximilian I. auf dem monumentalen Kenotaph in der Hofkirche, umgeben von den 28 „Schwarzen Mandern“ (und Frauen). Sie bewachen allerdings ein leeres Grab: Auf seinem Totenbett entschied Maximilian, dass er nicht in Innsbruck, sondern in seiner Taufkapelle in Wiener Neustadt begraben werden sollte. Die Bronzefiguren, die Maximilian selbst in Auftrag gegeben hatte, waren für diese Kapelle – die im Obergeschoß der Burg liegt – allerdings zu schwer. Also entschied Maximilians Enkel Ferdinand I., in Innsbruck eine eigene Grabeskirche für Maximilian zu errichten.

MONUMENT FOR AN ABSENTEE *Emperor Maximilian I, cast in bronze, kneels here humbly on the monumental cenotaph in the Court Church, surrounded by the 28 "Schwarze Mander" [black men], (and women). However, they are guarding an empty grave. On his deathbed Maximilian decided that he should not be buried in Innsbruck, but in his baptistery in Wiener Neustadt. However the bronze figures that Maximilian himself had commissioned were too heavy for this chapel, which is on the top floor of the castle. So Maximilian's grandson, Ferdinand I, decided to establish an individual chapel for Maximilian in Innsbruck.*

Einmal im Jahr, am Totensonntag nach Allerheiligen, erstrahlen die „Schwarzen Mander“ im Kerzenschein.

Once a year, on Totensonntag [Sunday of the Dead] after All Saints, the “Schwarze Mander” are lit by candlelight.

In der „Silbernen Kapelle“, die der Hofkirche angeschlossen ist, befinden sich die Grabmäler von Ferdinand II. und seiner Gattin Philippine Welser.

The tombs of Ferdinand II and his wife Philippine Welser are located in the "Silberne Kapelle" [silver chapel] which is connected to the Court Church.

Im Dom zu St. Jakob erinnert ein monumentales Grabmal an Erzherzog Maximilian III. den Deutschmeister.

In St. James' Cathedral, a monumental tomb serves as memorial to Archduke Maximilian III, the Deutschmeister.

2.657 vergoldete Kupferschindeln bedecken das Goldene Dachl – das Prunkstück der Innsbrucker Altstadt.

2,657 gilded copper tiles cover the Golden Roof, the show-piece of Innsbruck's Old Town.

RÄTSELHAFTE INSCHRIFT Hinter dem Goldenen Dachl, der berühmtesten Sehenswürdigkeit der Stadt, verbirgt sich auch eines ihrer größten Mysterien: Auf Reliefsteinen entlang der Brüstung findet man seltsame Schriftzeichen, die entfernt an hebräische Buchstaben erinnern. Ihre Bedeutung ist bis heute umstritten: Handelt es sich um eine Fantasieschrift, die das mystische Flair des Orients heraufbeschwören sollte? Oder wollte uns Maximilian I. eine verschlüsselte Botschaft zukommen lassen? Einen besonders originellen Versuch der Deutung unternahm 2009 die Wiener „schule für dichtung“: Ihrem Aufruf, kreative Übersetzungen dieses rätselhaften Textes zu schreiben, folgten zahlreiche Teilnehmer mit zum Teil äußerst fantasievollen Beiträgen.

ENIGMATIC INSCRIPTION *Behind the Golden Roof, the most famous landmark of the city, one of its greatest mysteries is also hidden. On relief panels along the parapet one can find strange characters, vaguely reminiscent of Hebrew letters. Their significance has remained controversial. Does it involve a fantasy font, invented to conjure up the mystical flair of the Orient? Or did Maximilian I wish to send us an encrypted message? The "vienna poetry school" undertook a highly original interpretation in 2009. The calling to write creative translations of this enigmatic text was taken up by numerous participants, resulting in some very imaginative contributions.*

Die gotischen Gewölbe hinter dem Goldenen Dachl bergen ein Museum zur Zeit Maximilians I.

The Gothic vault behind the Golden Roof houses a museum about the days of Maximilian I.

Die Triumphpforte am südlichen Ende der Maria-Theresien-Straße wird von einem Reliefbild gekrönt, das Kaiserin Maria Theresia und ihren Gatten Kaiser Franz I. Stephan zeigt.

The Triumphal Arch at the southern end of Maria-Theresien-Straße is crowned with a relief image, which portrays the Empress Maria Theresa and her husband, Emperor Franz I Stephan.

Der Rudolfsbrunnen am Bozner Platz wurde aus Anlass von 500 Jahren Zugehörigkeit Tirols zum Habsburgerreich errichtet.

The Rudolf Fountain on Boznerplatz was erected to celebrate the 500 th anniversary of Tyrol's entry into the Habsburg Empire.

FREUD UND LEID 1765 herrschte große Freude in Innsbruck: Erzherzog Leopold, Sohn Kaiserin Maria Theresias, sollte hier seine Verlobte Maria Ludovica heiraten, die kaiserliche Familie für längere Zeit in der Stadt residieren. Zur Feier dieses Anlasses ließ man einen Triumphbogen errichten, durch den das Brautpaar in die Stadt einzog. Doch inmitten der Hochzeitsfeierlichkeiten starb Leopolds Vater Franz Stephan. Die Triumphpforte (siehe vorige Doppelseite), ursprünglich aus Holz und Gips gestaltet und erst Jahre später aus Stein neu erbaut, erinnert an die beiden so gegensätzlichen Ereignisse.

JOY AND SORROW *1765 was a time of great joy in Innsbruck. Archduke Leopold, son of Empress Maria Theresa, was to marry his fiancée, Maria Ludovica, and the imperial family was to reside in the city for a long time. In celebration of this event, the Triumphal Arch was built through which the couple entered the city. However, in the midst of the wedding festivities, Leopold's father, Franz Stephan, died. The Triumphal Arch (see previous double page), originally constructed of wood and plaster and only rebuilt years later from stone, is reminiscent of the two opposing events.*

Den Leopoldsbrunnen gegenüber der Hofburg krönt ein Bronzestandbild von Erzherzog Leopold V. auf dem Rücken seines Pferdes.

The Leopold Fountain opposite the Imperial Palace is crowned by a bronze statue of Archduke Leopold V on the back of his horse.

Kaiser Maximilian I. ließ das Zeughaus weit außerhalb der Stadtmauern als Waffenarsenal errichten – heute beherbergt das Gebäude ein Museum zur Kulturgeschichte Tirols.

Emperor Maximilian I had the armoury built far outside the city walls as an arsenal – the building now houses a museum on the cultural history of Tyrol.

Schloss Ambras, einer der schönsten Renaissancebauten nördlich der Alpen.

Ambras Castle, one of the most beautiful Renaissance buildings north of the Alps.

Die Fassaden im Innenhof des Ambraser Hochschlosses sind mit Grisaillemalereien überzogen, die den plastischen Eindruck von Reliefs erwecken.

The façades of the courtyard of the upper Ambras Castle are covered with grisaille paintings which evoke the vivid impression of a relief.

Über die Rüstkammern von Schloss Ambras wacht ein Heer von Rittern in Harnischen.

An army of knights in armour watch over the armouries of Ambras Castle.

WUNDERWELT Ferdinand von Tirol war ein leidenschaftlicher Sammler. Neben Gemälden, Büchern und Rüstungen sammelte er für seine „Kunst- und Wunderkammer" Ungewöhnliches aus aller Welt: einen Turban und einen Samuraiharnisch, einen Tafelaufsatz aus Rhinozeroshorn und ein Korallenkabinett, ausgestopfte Tiere und antike Skulpturen, Kunsthandwerk aus Perlmutt, Elfenbein, Bergkristall und Gold, Schnitzereien wie das „Tödlein", ein Porträt des Hofriesen Bartlmä Bon mit dem Hofzwerg Thomele und ein anderes von Vlad III., dem historischen Vorbild Draculas – ein Kuriositätenkabinett, das Ferdinands Gäste in Staunen versetzen und die Weltgewandtheit des Schlossherrn demonstrieren sollte.

WORLD OF WONDERS *Ferdinand of Tyrol was a passionate collector. In addition to paintings, books and armour, he collected unusual items for his "Kunst- und Wunderkammer" [chamber of art and curiosities] from around the world. These included: a turban and samurai armour, a table centrepiece made from rhinoceros horn, a coral cabinet, stuffed animals, ancient sculptures, arts and crafts from mother of pearl, ivory, rock crystal and gold, carvings such as the "Tödlein" [Shrine of Little Death], a portrait of the court giant Bartlmä Bon with the court dwarf Thomele, and another of Vlad III who was the historical inspiration for Dracula. It was a cabinet of curiosities that amazed Ferdinand's guests and was intended to demonstrate the worldly sophistication of the lord of the castle.*

Die Porträts im Spanischen Saal auf Schloss Ambras zeigt die Tiroler Landesfürsten von Graf Albrecht I. bis zu Ferdinand II., dem Bauherrn des Festsaals.

The portrait gallery of the Spanish Hall at Schloss Ambras shows the Tyrolean Princes from Count Albert I up to Ferdinand II, the builder of the ballroom.

Antike Skulpturen ...

Ancient sculptures ...

... und das filigrane „Tödlein“ in der „Kunst- und Wunderkammer“.

... and the filigree “Tödlein” [Shrine of Little Death] in the “chamber of art and curiosities”.

DOM

Der Dom zu St. Jakob, seit 1964 Bischofssitz der Diözese Innsbruck.

St. James' Cathedral, the bishop's see of the diocese of Innsbruck since 1964.

Städtische Glaubenswelten

Tirol pflegt traditionell eine besondere Beziehung zum Christentum – nicht umsonst singt das Andreas-Hofer-Lied vom „heil'gen Land Tirol". In der Gegenwart des 21. Jahrhunderts hat sich das Verhältnis zur Religion wie zur Kirche zwar verändert, neue Glaubensgemeinschaften wie der Islam oder die Kirchen des slawischen Raums haben an Bedeutung gewonnen. Im Stadtbild von Innsbruck ist die christliche Tradition aber unübersehbar: 52 öffentlich zugängliche Kapellen und Kirchen (darunter zwei evangelische) stehen den Gläubigen offen. Daneben findet man zahllose Wegkreuze, Marterln und Heiligenbilder als Zeichen traditioneller Frömmigkeit.

Besonders häufig trifft man in Innsbruck auf ein Marienbild, das Lucas Cranach d. Ä. vermutlich 1537 gemalt hat. Cranach war ein enger Freund Martin Luthers, der die verklärende Darstellung Marias im Katholizismus kritisiert hatte. So gestaltete Cranach ein neues, „protestantisches" Marienbild: eine einfache, schlicht gekleidete Frau aus dem Volk, die ihr nacktes Kind im Arm hält. Ursprünglich befand sich das Gemälde in Dresden, unter Erzherzog Leopold V. kam es nach Innsbruck und wurde der Stadtpfarrkirche St. Jakob, dem heutigen Dom, übergeben. Dort bildet dieses Mariahilf-Gnadenbild seither, umgeben von einem goldenen Strahlenkranz, den Mittelpunkt des prunkvollen Barockaltars und wurde als Inbegriff katholischer Marienverehrung vielfach kopiert – in Kapellen und Kirchen ebenso wie an über 100 Hausfassaden in der ganzen Stadt.

Die „Keimzelle" des kirchlichen Innsbruck befindet sich aber nicht in der Altstadt, sondern in Wilten: Bereits im 6. Jahrhundert stand hier, in der römischen Siedlung Veldidena, eine schlichte Holzkirche, aus der sich die heutige Basilika entwickelte. In unmittelbarer Nachbarschaft befindet sich die barocke Stiftskirche, Zentrum des 1138 gegründeten Prämonstratenserklosters.

Auch abseits dieser Prunkstücke, zu denen weiters der Dom und die Hofkirche zählen, bietet Innsbruck eine abwechslungsreiche Kirchenlandschaft: schlichte Dorfkirchen, Wallfahrtskapellen wie Heiligwasser und das Höttinger Bild oder auch viele moderne Bauten. Beinahe die Hälfte der Innsbrucker Kirchen stammt aus dem 20. Jahrhundert – von der neoromanischen Pfarrkirche in Altpradl bis zur „Kunstkirche" in Sieglanger.

Neben den christlichen Kirchen sind heute zahlreiche weitere Religionsgemeinschaften in Tirol beheimatet. Die traditionsreichste unter ihnen ist das Judentum: Seit dem 13. Jahrhundert gibt es in Innsbruck eine jüdische Gemeinde, seit 1993 verfügt sie wieder über eine Synagoge in der Sillgasse – ein unverzichtbarer Bestandteil der religiösen Vielfalt im modernen Innsbruck. ■

Der Schein trügt: Das aufwändig geschnitzte barocke Holzgehäuse auf der Empore des Innsbrucker Doms birgt eine moderne Orgel, die im Jahr 2000 eingeweiht wurde.

Appearances are deceiving: The elaborately carved baroque wooden cabinet in the gallery of St. James' Cathedral houses a modern organ, which was inaugurated in the year 2000.

World Faiths in the City

Tyrol traditionally maintains a special relationship with Christianity – it is no coincidence that the "Andreas-Hofer-Lied" speaks of the "holy land of Tyrol". Today in the 21st century the relationship to religion, as well as the Church has changed. New faiths such as Islam or the Slavic churches have gained in importance. Nonetheless the influence of the Christian tradition on the cityscape remains clearly visible: fifty-two publicly accessible chapels and churches (including two Protestant) are open to the faithful. In addition, you will find countless roadside crosses, shrines and sacred images as a sign of traditional piety.

In Innsbruck one frequently encounters one particular depiction of the Virgin Mary, painted by Lucas Cranach the Elder, presumably in 1537. Cranach was a close friend of Martin Luther, who had criticised the transfiguring representation of Mary in Catholicism. So Cranach designed a new "Protestant" picture of the Virgin Mary: a simple, plainly dressed woman of the people, holding her naked child in her arms. Originally the painting was located in Dresden. However, under Archduke Leopold V it came to Innsbruck and was handed over to the parish church of St. James, todays St. James' Cathedral. This miraculous image of the Madonna, surrounded by a golden halo, has since formed the centre of the magnificent baroque altar and has been copied many times as the epitome of Catholic devotion to Mary – in chapels and churches, as well as on more than 100 house façades throughout the city.

The "nucleus" of religious Innsbruck, however, is not found in the Old City, but in Wilten: Already in the 6th century, in the Roman settlement of Veldidena, a simple wooden church stood here and over time, developed into today's basilica. Situated in the immediate vicinity is the baroque Stiftskirche, the centre of the Premonstratensian monastery, founded in 1138.

Besides these show-pieces, which also include the Cathedral and the Court Church, Innsbruck offers a varied landscape of churches: simple village churches, pilgrim chapels such as Heiligwasser and the Höttinger Bild, as well as many more modern buildings. Almost half of the churches in Innsbruck date back to the 20th century – from the neo-Romanesque parish church in Altpradl to the "Kunstkirche" in Sieglanger.

In addition to the Christian churches there are numerous other religious communities located in Tyrol today. The most traditional of these is Judaism: since the 13th century there has been a Jewish community in Innsbruck. Since 1993 there is a synagogue in Sillgasse again – an essential part of the religious diversity in modern-day Innsbruck. ■

An die Jesuitenkirche, die alte Universitätskirche Innsbrucks, schließt sich das Gebäude der Theologischen Fakultät an.

The Jesuit Church, the old university church in Innsbruck, is joined to the building of the Faculty of Theology.

Die Spitalskirche in der Maria-Theresien-Straße trägt ihren Namen nach dem Heilig-Geist-Spital, in dem schon im 14. Jahrhundert die Kranken Innsbrucks kuriert und versorgt wurden.

The Spitalskirche [hospital church] on Maria-Theresien-Straße is named after the Heilig-Geist-Spital [Holy Ghost hospital], where the sick and injured of Innsbruck were cured and taken care of as early as the 14th century.

Der schlanke Turm der Servitenkirche überragt die Häuser entlang der Maria-Theresien-Straße.

The slender tower of the Servitenkirche [Servite Church] towers above the houses along Maria-Theresien-Straße.

Im Innenhof des Alten
Landhauses versteckt sich die
zierliche Georgskapelle.

The courtyard of the old Landhaus [Seat of the Tyrolean Government] is home to the elegant George's Chapel.

Die im neuromanischen Stil erbaute Herz-Jesu-Kirche ist Zentrum der Redemptoristen – und der kroatischen Gläubigen in Innsbruck.

Built in neo-Romanesque style, the Herz-Jesu-Kirche [Sacred Heart Church] is the centre of the Redemptorists and the Croatian believers in Innsbruck.

Im Stadtteil Pradl liegt der Militärfriedhof, der auf das Jahr 1931 zurückgeht.

The military cemetery, which dates back to 1931, is located in Pradl.

Der städtische Westfriedhof:
ein Ort der Stille und der Besinnung.

*The municipal West Cemetery:
a place of silence and contemplation.*

KRIEGERISCHER GEDÄCHTNISORT Einst war der Tummelplatz der Reitplatz von Schloss Ambras, wo die Pferde „getummelt“, also zugeritten wurden. In den Kriegsjahren zwischen 1797 und 1806 wurde Schloss Ambras als Lazarett genutzt, und die verstorbenen Soldaten wurden auf dem Tummelplatz beigesetzt. So entstand, mitten in der Idylle einer Waldlichtung, eine Gedenkstätte, die heute auch an die Gefallenen der Bergiselschlachten von 1809 und besonders der Weltkriege des 20. Jahrhunderts erinnert.

PLACE OF MILITARY REMEMBRANCE *The Tummelplatz [stomping ground] was once the riding area of Ambras Castle, where the horses "romped" or were broken in. During the war years between 1797 and 1806, Ambras Castle was used as a military hospital and the dead soldiers were buried in the Tummelplatz. Thus, in the midst of an idyllic clearing, a memorial site developed. Today it also commemorates those who fell in the Bergiselschlachten [Bergisel battles] of 1809 and the world wars of the 20th century.*

Schlichte Holzkreuze erinnern an die gefallenen Soldaten am Friedhof Tummelplatz.

Simple wooden crosses serve as remembrance of the fallen soldiers in the Tummelplatz Cemetery.

Der neue jüdische Friedhof Innsbrucks ist in den Westfriedhof integriert.

The new Jewish Cemetery in Innsbruck is integrated into the West Cemetery.

Pfarrkirche Igls
Hl. Messen
Samstag 19
Sonntag 10
19
Mittwoch 19
Freitag 19

Als klassische Dorfkirchen erinnern die Pfarrkirchen von Igls (links) und Amras (rechts) an die eigenständige Geschichte der ehemaligen Dörfer, die erst im 20. Jahrhundert eingemeindet wurden.

As classic village churches, the parish churches of Igls (left) and Amras (right) remind one of the independent history of the former villages, which were only incorporated in the 20th century.

DER GELÄUTERTE RIESE Der Riese Haymon, so erzählt die Sage, tötete seinen Konkurrenten Thyrsus in einem blutigen Kampf. Als er vor der Leiche seines Gegners stand, überkam Haymon allerdings Reue, er bekehrte sich zum Christentum und begann den Bau eines Klosters. Einen Drachen, der ihn bei dieser Arbeit störte, tötete er kurzerhand. Danach vollendete er den Bau des Klosters Wilten, wo heute noch eine Statue an den sagenhaften Klostergründer erinnert.

THE REFORMED GIANT *The giant Haymon, so legend tells, killed his competitor Thyrsus in a bloody battle. As he stood over the body of his opponent, Haymon was overcome by remorse. He converted to Christianity and began the construction of a monastery. He killed a dragon who was bothering him on the spot. After that he completed the construction of the Wilten Monastery, where a statue serves as reminder of the legendary founder of the monastery to this day.*

Goldener Schmuck auf schwarzem Holz, so schließt der barocke Hochaltar das Hauptschiff der Wiltener Stiftskirche ab.

With its golden adornment on black wood, the high altar completes the Baroque nave of Wilten Abbey Church.

Als Beweis seiner Heldentat hält der hölzerne Riese Haymon die Zunge des getöteten Drachens in der Hand.

As proof of his heroic prowess, the wooden giant Haymon holds the tongue of the slain dragon in his hand.

Die Wiltener Stiftskirche ist eines der Prunkstücke des Barock in Innsbruck.

The Wilten Abbey Church is one of the show-pieces of Baroque architecture in Innsbruck.

In Sichtweite der Stiftskirche liegt die Basilika „Unsere Liebe Frau unter den vier Säulen“ in Wilten, deren Zentrum eine strahlenumkränzte Madonnenstatue bildet.

Within sight of the abbey church is the basilica of "Unsere Liebe Frau unter den vier Säulen" [Our Lady under the four pillars] in Wilten, whose centre is formed by a statue of the Madonna emanating rays of light.

DIE SIEBENSCHLÄFERGROTTE In der Wallfahrtskirche von Schloss Mentlberg, nahe dem Innsbrucker Tierheim, wird nicht nur zu „Maria auf der Gallwiese“ gebetet, sondern auch zu den „Sieben Schläfern von Ephesus“: Der Legende zufolge sollen sieben junge Männer in der Zeit der Christenverfolgung um 250 in einer Höhle eingemauert worden sein. Als die Höhle 200 Jahre später wieder geöffnet wurde, habe man die Männer jedoch nicht tot, sondern lediglich schlafend vorgefunden. In der Kirche von Mentlberg erinnert eine krippenartige Grotte an die „Sieben Schläfer“, die als Fürsprecher bei hohem Fieber und „Todesschlaf“ angerufen werden.

THE SEVEN SLEEPERS' GROTTO *In the pilgrimage church of Mentlberg Castle, near Innsbruck's animal shelter, it is not only "Mary on the Gallwiese" who is prayed to, but also the "Seven Sleepers of Ephesus". According to legend, seven young men are said to have been walled into a cave during the time of the persecution of Christians at around 250 AD. When the cave was opened 200 years later, the men were purportedly found, not dead but merely sleeping. In the church of Mentlberg, a crib-like grotto recalls the "Seven Sleepers" who are called upon as intercessors in cases of high fever and "the sleep of death".*

Die Siebenschläfergrotte in der Kirche von Mentlberg.

The Seven Sleepers' Grotto in the Church of Mentlberg.

Die Waldkapelle Höttinger Bild ist ein beliebtes Wallfahrtsziel – unter anderem von Studenten, die hier Beistand suchen.

The Höttinger Bild is a popular pilgrimage destination – among others students seek counsel here.

Um der stark wachsenden Bevölkerung des Stadtteils eine religiöse Heimat zu bieten, wurde zu Beginn des 20. Jahrhunderts in Pradl eine neue Pfarrkirche errichtet.

In order to offer the rapidly growing population of the district a religious home a new parish church was built at the beginning of the 20th century in Pradl.

Mächtig erhebt sich die neugotische Pfarrkirche St. Nikolaus über die umliegenden Wohnhäuser.

The neo-Gothic parish church of St. Nikolaus rises imposingly over the surrounding houses.

Die Christus-Kirche im Stadtteil Saggen ist Zentrum der evangelischen Gemeinde Innsbrucks.

The Christ Church in Saggen is the centre of the Protestant community in Innsbruck.

In Hötting wurde 1909 bis 1911 eine neue Pfarrkirche errichtet, da der Vorgängerbau nicht genügend Platz für alle Gläubigen bot.

A new parish church was built in Hötting between 1909 and 1911, as the previous building did not offer enough space for the entire congregation.

Die Mariahilf-Kirche nördlich des Inns wurde aufgrund eines Gelöbnisses der Tiroler Landstände während des Dreißigjährigen Krieges erbaut.

The Mariahilf Church north of the Inn was built after a pledge was made by the Tyrolean state diet during the Thirty Years' War.

Die den Heiligen Ingenuin und Albuin geweihte Alte Pfarrkirche von Hötting geht bis auf das 13. Jahrhundert zurück.

The old parish church of Hötting, which was consecrated to the saints Ingenuin and Albuin, dates back to the 13th century.

TIROLER PASSION 60.000 Ziegel, von den Gläubigen gespendet und zu Fuß auf die Hungerburg geschleppt, waren erforderlich, um 1932 die Theresienkirche zu errichten. Der Neubau war nötig geworden, weil die alte Notkirche, ein Gartenhaus, dem Ansturm der Wallfahrer nicht mehr gewachsen war. Gut ein Jahrzehnt später war die Theresienkirche Schauplatz eines Kunstskandals: Die Fresken von Max Weiler, auf denen ein Soldat in Tiroler Landestracht dem gekreuzigten Jesus eine Lanze ins Herz sticht, sorgten für Empörung und mussten von der Polizei vor der Zerstörung geschützt und auf Anordnung des Vatikans verhüllt werden.

TYROLEAN PASSION *60,000 bricks, donated by the faithful and dragged by foot to the Hungerburg were needed in order to build the Theresienkirche [Theresa church] in 1932. The new building became necessary because the old temporary church, a garden shed, was no longer adequate for the rush of pilgrims who arrived. Over a decade later, the Theresienkirche [Theresa church] was the scene of an art scandal. The frescoes by Max Weiler, on which a soldier in traditional Tyrolean costume pierces the heart of the crucified Jesus with a lance, incited an uproar and had to be protected by the police from destruction and veiled by order of the Vatican.*

AM SCHÄDELBERG Eines der eindrucksvollsten Zeugnisse der Volksfrömmigkeit sind die sogenannten Kalvarienberge. Diese „Schädelberge" (vom lateinischen Wort *calvaria*) sind dem biblischen Golgota nachempfunden, der Hinrichtungsstätte Jesu vor den Toren Jerusalems. Dieser Tradition begegnet man auch im Stadtteil Arzl: Entlang von sieben Kreuzwegkapellen führt ein Weg einen kleinen Hügel empor zu einem achteckigen Kirchlein.

ON CALVARY *One of the most impressive testimonies of popular piety is the so-called Calvary (from the Latin word calvaria). These "Schädelberge" are modelled after the biblical Golgotha, the place of execution of Jesus at the gates of Jerusalem. This tradition is also encountered in Arzl. There, one finds seven Stations of The Cross where a path leads up to a small octagonal church, which crowns a small hill.*

Die Pfarrkirche von Mühlau bildet das Zentrum dieses Stadtteils, der bis heute seinen dörflichen Charakter bewahrt hat.

The parish church of Mühlau forms the centre of this district, which has retained its village character up to this day.

Der Kalvarienberg bei Arzl.

The Calvary at Arzl.

Der kleine Pestfriedhof in Hötting geht auf eine Pestepidemie im Jahr 1625 zurück.

The small Plague Cemetery in Hötting dates back to a plague epidemic in 1625.

SPRUNGSCHANZE GOTTES Die 1962 geweihte Kirche „Maria am Gestade“ in Sieglanger stellt eine besonders geglückte Verbindung von moderner Kirchenarchitektur und Bildender Kunst dar. Einige der bedeutendsten zeitgenössischen Künstler des Landes haben an dem Bau mitgewirkt, so unter anderem Max Weiler (Betonglaswand), Rudolf Wach (Tabernakel) und Rudolf Millonig (Altar). Die Architektur des von Karl Rappold geplanten Baus hat dagegen seinen volkstümlichen Spitznamen inspiriert: Wegen ihres elegant geschwungenen Dachs, das an einen hohen Glockenturm anschließt, wird die Kirche auch „Sprungschanze Gottes“ genannt.

SKI JUMP OF GOD *The church "Maria am Gestade" [Mary on the Strand], which was consecrated in 1962, in Sieglanger represents a particularly successful combination of modern church architecture and the visual arts. Some of the most important contemporary artists in the country participated in the construction. Among others, Max Weiler (concrete glass wall), Rudolf Wach (tabernacle) and Rudolf Millonig (altar). The popular nickname was inspired by the architecture of the construction designed by Karl Rappold. This is due to its elegantly curved roof, reminiscent of a high bell tower. The church is also called the "Sprungschanze Gottes" [Ski Jump of God].*

Zwei Zeugnisse moderner Kirchenarchitektur: Die Pfarrkirche Sieglanger (oben und linke Seite) und die von Clemens Holzmeister geplante Pfarrkirche Allerheiligen (unten).

Two examples of modern church architecture: The Sieglanger parish church (above and left) and the parish church of Allerheiligen, designed by Clemens Holzmeister (below).

SPORTALM

Selbstbewusste Bürgerstadt

Viele der kulturgeschichtlichen „Highlights" von Innsbruck gehen zwar auf die Initiative von Bauherren aus Kirche und Hof zurück – das Stadtbild von Innsbruck aber haben seine Bürger über Jahrhunderte hinweg gestaltet.

Bereits während des späten Mittelalters, als mit der Hofburg, der Hofkirche und dem Goldenen Dachl Schaustücke höfischer Pracht entstanden, erlebte Innsbruck auch eine erste Hochblüte bürgerlicher Kultur. Die Stadtbevölkerung profitierte von Innsbrucks Erhebung zur Residenzstadt ab 1420 – sichtbares Zeichen dieses Aufschwungs ist der stolze Stadtturm, der an das alte Rathaus angebaut wurde. Anstelle der alten, oft noch aus Holz errichteten Gebäuden entstanden reiche gotische Bürgerhäuser in der Altstadt sowie in Mariahilf und St. Nikolaus am gegenüberliegenden Innufer.

Um den begrenzten Platz innerhalb der Stadtmauern bestmöglich auszunutzen, stattete man viele Häuser mit Erkern aus und errichtete offene Gewölbegänge, auf die man die oberen Stockwerke aufsetzte – diese Laubengänge tragen bis heute zum besonderen Charme der Innsbrucker Altstadt bei.

500 Jahre später gab der Bauboom der Gründerzeitjahre in der zweiten Hälfte des 19. Jahrhunderts der Innsbrucker Innenstadt ihre gegenwärtige Gestalt. Nicht zuletzt durch den Anschluss an das Eisenbahnnetz – 1858 wurde Innsbruck mit München verbunden, 1867 wurde die Brennerbahn eröffnet, 1884 die Arlbergbahn – erlebte die Stadt einen ungeheuren Aufschwung. Handel und Tourismus florierten, die Industrialisierung brachte ein wohlhabendes Bürgertum hervor und ließ die Einwohnerzahl rasant wachsen:

Zwischen 1842 und 1900 verdreifachte sich die Stadtbevölkerung beinahe und näherte sich um die Jahrhundertwende der 50.000er-Marke. Ganze Straßenzüge wurden im Baustil des Historismus umgestaltet, in Wilten und Pradl wurden großzügige Häuserblocks errichtet, um Wohnraum für die Menschen zu schaffen, die auf der Suche nach Arbeit in die Stadt strömten, und im Saggen entstand auf dem Reißbrett ein Villenviertel.

Das bürgerliche Selbstbewusstsein dieser Epoche spiegeln auch zahlreiche öffentliche Gebäude, mit denen das Bürgertum seinen Führungsanspruch nicht nur in wirtschaftlicher Hinsicht, sondern auch auf dem Gebiet der Verwaltung, der Bildung und der Kultur untermauerte.

Diese Tradition ist bis heute lebendig: Innsbruck ist mit Rathaus und Landhaus Sitz einer modernen Administration, gleichzeitig Zentrum der Bildung und des wissenschaftlichen Fortschritts, der an der Klinik ebenso stattfindet wie an den Instituten der Universität. Und zwischen Theatern und Museen, Galerien und Kleinkunstbühnen entfaltet sich ein vielfältiges Angebot, das Innsbruck den Rang einer Kulturstadt von überregionalem Format verleiht. ■

Confident bourgeois city

Although many of the cultural-historical "highlights" of Innsbruck can be traced back to the initiative of the owners of the Church and the Court – the cityscape of Innsbruck, however, has been created by its citizens over the centuries.

Already during the late Middle Ages, when show-pieces of courtly splendour emerged with the Imperial Palace, the Court Church and the Golden Roof, Innsbruck experienced its first heyday of bourgeois culture. The city's population benefited from Innsbruck's promotion to a seat of royal power from 1420 onwards. A visible sign of this boom is the lordly City Tower, which was attached to the old Town Hall. Instead of the old and often still wooden buildings, rich Gothic town houses were built in the Old Town as well as in Mariahilf and St. Nikolaus on the opposite Inn bank.

In order to utilise the limited space within the city walls as well as possible, many houses were fitted with oriels. Open vaulted passages were constructed, upon which one could build the upper floors – until this day these arcades contribute to the charm of the Old Town of Innsbruck.

Five hundred years later the building boom of the Gründerzeit [promoterism] in the second half of the 19th century provided Innsbruck's inner city with its present form. Not least due to the connection to the railway network. In 1858 Innsbruck was connected with Munich, in 1867 the Brenner railway was opened and in 1884 the Arlberg railway. The city experienced a huge upswing. Trade and tourism flourished, industrialisation spawned a prosperous middle class and enabled the population to grow rapidly:

Between 1842 and 1900 the city's population nearly tripled, approaching 50,000 inhabitants at the turn of the century. Whole streets were redesigned in the style of Historicism. In Wilten and Pradl generous residential blocks were erected in order to provide housing for the people who flocked to the city in search of work and in Saggen an elegant residential area was created from scratch.

The self-confident bourgeoisie of this period is also reflected in a number of public buildings with which the bourgeoisie reinforced its claim to leadership not only in economic terms, but also in the field of management, education and culture. This tradition is still alive today:

With the City Hall and the Landhaus [Seat of the Tyrolean Government], Innsbruck houses a modern administration, and is simultaneously the centre of education and scientific progress, which takes place at the hospital, as well as at the institutes of the university. And what with theatres and museums, galleries and cabaret, a wide range of possibilities unfolds, which raises Innsbruck to the rank of a city of culture on a national level. ■

Wie aus Zuckerguss: Gegenüber des Goldenen Dachls zeigt das Helblinghaus seine üppige Fassade.

As if made of icing: Opposite the Golden Roof the Helblinghaus displays its exuberant façade.

Historische Wirtshausschilder in der Altstadt erinnern an die lange Tradition der Innsbrucker Gastfreundlichkeit.

Historic inn signs in the Old Town are reminiscent of the long tradition of hospitality in Innsbruck.

Die Ottoburg, einst ein Wehrturm, beherbergt heute ein bodenständiges Gasthaus.

The Ottoburg, once a defence tower, now houses a down to earth inn.

Als äußeres Zeichen des bürgerlichen Selbstbewusstseins überragt der Innsbrucker Stadtturm die Häuser der Altstadt.

As an outward sign of bourgeois self-confidence, the Innsbruck City Tower dominates the houses of the Old Town.

UNGEWÖHNLICHES WAPPENTIER In den Lauben der Innsbrucker Altstadt begegnet man einem besonderen Tier: Der Quaternionenadler stand zur Zeit Maximilians I. als Symbol für das Heilige Römische Reich und seine vier Säulen. Die Verbindung des doppelköpfigen Adlers – Zeichen für das Kaisertum – mit einem Kruzifix verweist auf die Verbindung zwischen weltlicher und geistlicher Macht. In Auftrag gegeben wurde dieses gotische Fresko von Walter Zeller, der 1495 von Maximilian zum Stadtrichter ernannt worden war. Zum Dank für diese Ehrung verzierte er sein Haus mit dem Symbol für Macht und Größe seines Herrn.

UNUSUAL EMBLEM *One can encounter a special animal in the arcades of Innsbruck's Old Town: the Quaternion Eagle stood as symbol for the Holy Roman Empire and its four pillars at the time of Maximilian I. The combination of the double-headed eagle, symbol of the empire, and a crucifix refers to the connection between temporal and spiritual power. The gothic fresco was commissioned by Walter Zeller, who had been appointed as town magistrate in 1495 by Maximilian. In gratitude for this honour he decorated his house with the symbol of the power and greatness of his Lord.*

Einer der zahlreichen historischen Brunnen der Altstadt im Innenhof des Alten Rathauses.

One of the many historic fountains of the Old Town in courtyard of the old Town Hall.

Mittels Strebebögen stützen einander die Häuser in den engen Altstadtgassen.

The houses support each other in the narrow old streets by means of flying buttresses.

Der doppeltürmige Dom überragt die
Altstadtfassaden zum Herzog-Otto-Ufer.

*The twin-towered Cathedral towers over the
Old Town walls towards the Herzog-Otto Ufer.*

Das Laubengewölbe
beim sogenannten
Zeller-Haus ziert der
Quaternionenadler.

*The Quaternion Eagle
adorns the vault of the
so-called Zeller house.*

Jedes Jahr im Dezember verleiht der traditionelle Christkindlmarkt der Innsbrucker Altstadt vorweihnachtlichen Glanz.

Every year in December, the traditional Christmas market gives the Old Town of Innsbruck a pre-christmas glow.

INSPRUCKE Der Name Innsbruck geht auf die erste hölzerne Brücke zurück, die um 1170 den Marktflecken nördlich des Inns – die Stadtteile Mariahilf und St. Nikolaus – mit dem südlichen Flussufer verband. Während heute ein Dutzend Brücken den Inn überspannen, war damals die historische Innbrücke weit und breit die einzige Möglichkeit, den Fluss zu überqueren, und damit von entscheidender Bedeutung für die Entwicklung der Stadt.

INSPRUCKE *The name Innsbruck dates back to the first wooden bridge which around 1170 linked the market towns north of the Inn, the districts of Mariahilf and St. Nikolaus, with the southern riverbank. Whereas today a dozen bridges span the Inn, back then the historic Inn Bridge was by far and wide the only way to cross the river, and thus of crucial importance for the development of the city.*

Die gotischen Fassaden von Mariahilf bilden das Gegenüber der Innsbrucker Altstadt am anderen Flussufer.

The gothic façades of Mariahilf form a contrast to the Innsbruck Old Town across the river.

Ein modernes Kruzifix des Bildhauers Rudi Wach steht heute auf der Innbrücke zur Altstadt.

Today a modern crucifix by the sculptor Rudi Wach stands on the Inn Bridge.

Der Waltherpark im Stadtteil St. Nikolaus ist Naherholungsgebiet für Groß und Klein.

The Walther Park in the district of St. Nikolaus is a recreational area for young and old.

IN DER KOATLACKN Noch bevor die Innsbrucker Altstadt entstand, existierte auf der gegenüberliegenden Flussseite die Siedlung „Anbruggen“, das heutige St. Nikolaus. Jahrhundertelang galt Anbruggen als „Armenhaus Innsbrucks“, wo viele Menschen auf engem Raum lebten. Da es keine Kanalisation gab, verwandelte sich die St.-Nikolaus-Gasse nach jedem stärkeren Regenfall in einen Sumpf, in dem die Abwässer zusammenflossen. Daher leitet sich der Name „Koatlackn“ ab, den die alteingesessenen Bewohner von St. Nikolaus bis heute mit einem gewissen Heimatstolz verwenden.

IN THE KOATLACKN *Even before the Old Town of Innsbruck came into being, the opposite side of the river held the settlement "Anbruggen", todays St. Nikolaus. For centuries Anbruggen was the "poorhouse of Innsbruck" where many people lived in a very small space. Since there were no sewers, after every heavy rainfall the St.-Nikolaus-Gasse transformed into a swamp into which the sewage flowed. It is from this occurrence that the name "Koatlackn" [Faeces Lake] is derived which has been used by the old-established residents of St. Nikolaus up until today, with some local pride.*

Der Emile-Bethouart-Steg verbindet St. Nikolaus mit der Innsbrucker Innenstadt.

The Emile-Bethouart-Steg connects St. Nikolaus with the city centre.

Am Annatag 1703 zogen die letzten bayerischen Truppen aus Tirol ab, die im Spanischen Erbfolgekrieg in das Land vorgestoßen waren. Zum Dank dafür errichteten die Tiroler Landstände 1706 die Annasäule in der Maria-Theresien-Straße.

On St Anne's day in 1703 the last Bavarian troops, who had entered the country during the War of Spanish Succesion, withdrew. In gratitude for this the Tyrolean Estates erected the Annasäule on Maria-Theresien-Straße in 1706.

Das von Georg Anton Gumpp errichtete Alte Landhaus zählt zu den schönsten Barockbauten in Innsbruck.

The old Landhaus [Seat of the Tyrolean Government] built by Georg Anton Gumpp is one of the most beautiful baroque buildings in Innsbruck.

Das Neue Landhaus ist das Zentrum der Regierung und Verwaltung des Landes.

The new Landhaus [Seat of the Tyrolean Government] is the centre of government and administration of the state.

INNSBRUCKER URGESTEIN Der Stein, aus dem die Stadt erbaut ist – diesen Titel könnte man ohne weiteres der Höttinger Brekzie verleihen: Zahlreichen Bauwerken in Innsbruck gibt dieser Stein ihr charakteristisches Aussehen, von der Triumphpforte bis zu den Hochwasserschutzmauern entlang des Inns, vom Dom bis zum Stadtturm und den Stützmauern an vielen Altstadthäusern. Schon im Mittelalter wurde die Brekzie in Steinbrüchen zwischen Hötting und Mühlau abgebaut: Sie ist leicht zu bearbeiten, widerstandsfähig und noch dazu in unmittelbarer Stadtnähe verfügbar – so wurde sie zum beliebtesten Baustein im Raum Innsbruck.

INNSBRUCK'S FOUNDATIONS *The stone from which the city is built – one could readily give the Höttinger Breccia this title – gives numerous buildings in Innsbruck their characteristic appearance: from the Triumphal Arch to the retaining walls along the Inn River, and from The Cathedral to the City Tower and the supporting walls of many of the Old Town's houses. The breccia was mined in quarries between Hötting and Mühlau as early as the Middle Ages. It is easy to cut, durable and moreover available close to the city. It therefore became the most popular building material in the Innsbruck area.*

Der Ansitz Wolkenstein, 1700 zum Barockpalais umgestaltet, befindet sich seit 1804 im Besitz der Grafen Trapp.

The Wolkenstein Residence, which was converted into a baroque palace in 1700, has been in the possession of the Counts Trapp since 1804.

Das Winklerhaus neben der Triumphpforte ist der wichtigste Jugendstilbau in der Innsbrucker Innenstadt.

The Winklerhaus next to the Triumphal Arch is the most important Art Nouveau building in the centre of Innsbruck.

LANDESTHEATER

Das Landestheater am Rennweg, das seine heutige Gestalt 1844 erhielt, bildet seit 1629 das Zentrum der Tiroler Schauspielkunst.

The State Theatre on the Rennweg, which assumed it's present day appearance in 1844, has been the centre of Tyrolean performing arts since 1629.

Die ehemalige Hauptpost (links) und die Bundesbahndirektion (rechts) demonstrieren das neue bürgerliche Selbstbewusstsein der Gründerzeitära.

The former main post office (left) and the railway directorate (right) demonstrate the emerging bourgeois self-confidence of the Gründerzeit [promoterism].

Elegante Fassaden im Gründerzeitstil säumen die Straßen im Saggen.

Elegant façades in the style of the Gründerzeit [promoterism] line the streets in Saggen.

Im Stil der 1970er Jahre wurde der Betonbau des Landesgerichts errichtet – ein monumentales Denkmal der Gerechtigkeit.

The concrete building of the State Court was built in the style of the 1970s – a huge monument of justice.

Im Saggen entstand im späten 19. Jahrhundert ein nobles Villenviertel für das Innsbrucker Bürgertum.

In the late 19th century a smart residential area was built for Innsbruck's bourgeoisie in Saggen.

Drei Stätten der Bildung in Innsbruck: Die ehemalige Gilmschule (oben), die Daniel-Sailer-Schule im Saggen (unten) und das Gebäude der Handelsakademie (rechts oben).

Three centres of education in Innsbruck: The former Gilmschule (above), the Daniel-Sailer-Schule (below) and the building of the Academy of Commerce (above right).

Die Rotunde am Fuß der alten Hungerburgbahn wurde als Ausstellungsort für das Riesenrundgemälde errichtet, das seit 2010 im Tirol Panorama am Bergisel zu sehen ist.

The rotunda at the foot of the old Hungerburg funicular was built as a venue for the Riesenrundgemälde [Panoramic Painting] which can be seen at the Tirol Panorama on Bergisel since 2010.

Im „Blocksaggen“ umgeben lange Reihen von Zinshäusern begrünte Innenhöfe.

In “Blocksaggen” long rows of apartment buildings surround landscaped courtyards.

MUSEUM
FERDINANDEUM
SCHOEPF
KAUFMANN

SAMMELFREUDEN Neben Wien ist Innsbruck Österreichs wichtigste Museumsstadt. Bedeutende historische Sammlungen findet man im Landesmuseum Ferdinandeum, das mit seinen Dependancen im Zeughaus, im Volkskunstmuseum und am Bergisel als „Gedächtnis des Landes" fungiert, sowie in den städtischen Museen im Stadtarchiv/Stadtmuseum und im Goldenen Dachl. Weniger bekannt, aber umso origineller sind die vielen kleinen, teils privat geführten Museen: die „Radiowelt", die 80 Jahre Radiogeschichte zeigt, das Localbahnmuseum im alten Stubaitalbahnhof oder das schaurig-faszinierende Anatomische Museum an der Klinik.

THE JOY OF COLLECTING *Alongside Vienna, Innsbruck is Austria's most important museum city. Significant historical collections can be found in the Ferdinandeum State Museum, which acts as the "memory of the state" with its branches in the Armoury, the Volkskunstmuseum [Folk Art Museum] and Bergisel, as well as in the municipal museums, the City Archives/ City Museum, and the Golden Roof. Less known, but all the more original, are the many small, mostly privately owned museums: The "Radio World", which displays 80 years of radio history, the local funicular museum in the old Stubaital train station, or the eerily fascinating Museum of Anatomy at the hospital.*

Das 1823 gegründete Landesmuseum Ferdinandeum beherbergt die wichtigste historische und kunstgeschichtliche Sammlung des Landes.

The Ferdinandeum State Museum, founded in 1823, is home to the most important historical and art collections in the state.

Das Landesmuseum Ferdinandeum lädt zu einer Zeitreise durch 30.000 Jahre – von Exponaten aus der Frühgeschichte bis zu moderner Kunst.

The Ferdinandeum State Museum invites visitors on a journey through 30,000 years with exhibits from prehistoric times right up to modern art.

Abfall.

Der „Verführer Luzifer“ begrüßt die Besucher des Tiroler Volkskunstmuseums.

The “Verführer Luzifer” [Deceiver Lucifer] welcomes visitors to the Tyrolean Volkskunstmuseum [Folk Art Museum].

Das Volkskunstmuseum befindet sich im Gebäude des Franziskanerklosters, das rund um den Kreuzgang angelegt ist.

The Volkskunstmuseum [Folk Art Museum] is located in the Franciscan monastery, which is arranged around a cloister.

Teil der umfangreichen Sammlung des Volkskunstmuseums sind Bauernstuben aus allen Regionen des Landes.

Part of the extensive collection of the Volkskunstmuseum [Folk Art Museum] are farmhouse parlours from all regions of the country.

Im Stadtarchiv/Stadtmuseum, dem „Langzeitgedächtnis“ Innsbrucks, ist auch das sehenswerte Stadtmuseum untergebracht.

The City Archives/City Museum, known as the “long-term memory” of Innsbruck, also house the most interesting City Museum.

Das Kaiserjägermuseum am Bergisel dokumentiert die Geschichte dieser historischen Infanterietruppe.

The Kaiserjägermuseum [Imperial Infantry Museum] on Bergisel documents the tale of this historical infantry troop.

Den Mittelpunkt der Anlagen am Bergisel bildet die überlebensgroße Statue Andreas Hofers.

The larger than life statue of Andreas Hofer was erected in the centre of Bergisel.

Das Urichhaus am Bergisel ist Sitz des Alt-Kaiserjäger-Clubs, der Aussichtspavillon (unten) erlaubt weite Blicke über die Stadt.

The Urichhaus on Bergisel is headquarters of the Old Imperial Hunting Club. The gazebo (below) offers extensive views over the city.

GESCHICHTE IM RUNDBLICK 1809 wurde am Innsbrucker Bergisel Geschichte geschrieben: Dreimal schlugen die Tiroler Truppen unter Andreas Hofer die französische und bayerische Übermacht zurück, erst in einer vierten Schlacht mussten sie sich geschlagen geben. Doch der Mythos vom mutigen Kampf der Tiroler, die sich voll Heimatstolz und Gottvertrauen den Feinden entgegenstellten, blieb lebendig: nicht zuletzt im Riesenrundgemälde, einer Panoramadarstellung der dritten Bergiselschlacht. 1896 wurde das Heldenpanorama erstmals in einem eigens dafür erbauten Gebäude im Saggen gezeigt, 2010 übersiedelte es an den Schauplatz des Geschehens am Bergisel.

HISTORY WITH A PANORAMIC VIEW *In 1809 history was made on the Bergisel. Under Andreas Hofer the Tyrolean troops repelled the superior French and Bavarian forces three times, only in a fourth battle were they forced to admit defeat. However, the myth of the courageous struggle of the Tyroleans, who confronted the enemy full of national pride and trust in God, remained alive. Not least in the Riesenrundgemälde, a panoramic portrayal of the third Bergisel battle. In 1896 the heroes' panorama was first shown in a purpose-built building in Saggen. In 2010 it was moved to the scene of the action on Bergisel.*

Das Museum Tirol Panorama ist seit 2010 Ausstellungsort des Riesenrundgemäldes.

Since 2010 the Riesenrundgemälde [panoramic painting] is on display at The Museum Tirol Panorama [The Tyrol Panorama Museum].

UNIVERS
LEOPOLDINO - FR

Das Hauptgebäude der Leopold-Franzens-Universität Innsbruck ist Sitz des Rektorats und der juridischen Fakultät.

The main building of the Leopold-Franzens-University of Innsbruck houses the rector's office and the Law Faculty.

Neben dem alten Hauptgebäude der Universität zählen der „Geiwi-Turm“ und das Bruno-Sander-Haus zum Campus am Innrain.

In addition to the old main building of the University, the “GeiWi Tower” and the Bruno-Sander-House are part of the Innrain Campus.

STADT IN DER STADT Mit über 30.000 Studierenden und über 6.000 Mitarbeitern haben die Universitäten Innsbrucks heute die Dimension einer Stadt innerhalb der Stadt. Die Anfänge waren bescheidener: 1669 wurde unter Kaiser Leopold I., finanziert durch eine Sondersteuer auf das Haller Salz, die erste Universität gegründet. Heute verteilen sich die 16 Fakultäten der Leopold-Franzens-Universität sowie die Medizinische Universität über das ganze Stadtgebiet. Die wichtigste Bildungs- und Forschungseinrichtung Westösterreichs hat Wissenschaftler von internationalem Rang hervorgebracht – unter anderem vier Nobelpreisträger für Chemie und Physik.

CITY WITHIN A CITY *With over 30,000 students and over 6,000 employees, the University of Innsbruck has today reached the dimensions of a city within a city. The beginnings were more modest. In 1669 under Emperor Leopold I, the first university was founded, financed by a special tax on salt from Hall. Today, the 16 faculties of the Leopold-Franzens-University, as well as the Medical University, are spread over the entire city. The most important educational and research institution in western Austria has created scientists of international standing. These include four Nobel Laureates in Chemistry and Physics.*

Heimat von ca. 3,5 Millionen Büchern: die Universitäts- und Landesbibliothek.

Home to around 3.5 million books: the University and State Library.

1969 entstand in Hötting West ein neuer Universitätscampus, auf dem naturwissenschaftliche und technische Institute untergebracht sind.

In 1969, a new university campus was created in Hötting West, in which the scientific and technical institutes are housed.

Neben der Jesuitenkirche befindet sich die Theologische Fakultät der Universität mit dem festlichen Kaiser-Leopold-Saal.

The Theological Faculty of the university, complete with the festive Kaiser-Leopold-Saal [Emperor Leopold Hall] is situated next to the Jesuit church.

IM TIERGARTEN Zwischen Fürstenweg und Flughafen befand sich einst ein Tiergarten: Kein Zoo im heutigen Sinn, sondern ein umzäuntes Jagdareal, auf dem Hirsche und Gämsen darauf warteten, von den adeligen Gästen des Landesherrn geschossen zu werden. Heute erinnern nicht nur manche Straßennamen in dieser Gegend – Tiergartenstraße, Rehgasse und Steinbockweg – daran, sondern auch der sogenannte Pulverturm: Einst als Jagdschlösschen errichtet, später als Munitionsdepot verwendet, ist er heute Teil des Universitätssportinstituts und beherbergt unter anderem eine Kletterhalle.

AT THE ZOO *Between Fürstenweg and the airport there was once a zoo. Not a zoo in the modern sense, but a fenced in hunting area where deer and chamois waited to be shot by the noble guests of the Lord. Today, not only some street names in this area, Tiergartenstraße [Zoo Street], Rehgasse [Deer Alley] and Steinbockweg [Ibex Path], serve as a reminder of this, but also the so-called Pulverturm [Powder Tower]. It was originally built as a hunting lodge and later used as an ammunition depot. It is now part of the University Sports Institute and houses, among other things, an indoor climbing wall.*

Der Flughafen in Kranebitten, der 1948 den alten Flughafen in der Reichenau ersetzte, ist Innsbrucks Tor zur Welt.

The airport in Kranebitten, which replaced the old one in the Reichenau in 1948, is Innsbruck's gateway to the world.

2002 wurde der Großteil der Innsbrucker Stadtverwaltung in dem von Dominique Perrault geplanten Neuen Rathaus zusammengefasst.

In 2002 the majority of Innsbruck's City Council relocated to the new Town Hall, designed by Dominique Perrault.

Stadt der Moderne

Das Stadtbild von Innsbruck befindet sich in einem stetigen Wandel. Insbesondere in der Innenstadt sind seit den 1990er Jahren zahlreiche Neubauten entstanden, die eine spannende, manchmal auch umstrittene Verbindung mit den historischen Bauwerken in ihrer Nachbarschaft eingehen.

Innsbrucks Beziehung zur modernen Architektur reicht aber deutlich weiter zurück: Bereits vor der Mitte des 20. Jahrhunderts wirkten bedeutende Architekten wie Franz Baumann (Seilbahnstationen der Nordkettenbahn), Clemens Holzmeister (Pfarrkirche Allerheiligen) oder Lois Welzenbacher (Adambräu-Sudhaus) in der Stadt.

Lois Welzenbacher war es auch, der Innsbruck in den 1920er Jahren sein erstes Hochhaus – der heutige Sitz der Innsbrucker Kommunalbetriebe – und damit einen frühen Architekturskandal bescherte. Überhaupt scheint moderne Architektur stets für öffentliche Auseinandersetzungen gut zu sein: Sie fanden zur Zeit Welzenbachers ebenso statt wie zu Beginn des 21. Jahrhunderts rund um die Neugestaltung des Innsbrucker Hauptbahnhofs oder des Kaufhauses Tyrol, das 2010 nach Plänen von David Chipperfield neu errichtet wurde.

Von Diskussionen über Möglichkeiten und Gefahren moderner Architektur war auch die Neuerrichtung des Innsbrucker Rathauses begleitet – ein eleganter Bau, dessen Glasfassaden symbolisch für eine offene, transparente Stadtpolitik stehen, und an dessen Gestaltung auch namhafte bildende Künstler wie Peter Kogler, Daniel Buren und Heinz Gappmayr mitgewirkt haben.

Moderne Architektur beschränkt sich aber nicht nur auf öffentliche Gebäude, zu denen auch Klinik, Universität, Museen oder der neue Innsbrucker Hauptbahnhof zählen; sie zeigt sich auch im Wohnbau: Vor allem an den Stadträndern entstanden im Verlauf der vergangenen Jahrzehnte zahlreiche Neubauten, die den Bedürfnissen ihrer Bewohner ebenso zu genügen versuchen wie den Ansprüchen zeitgemäßer Architektur.

Die spektakulärsten Spuren im Erscheinungsbild des modernen Innsbruck hat wohl die britisch-irakische Architektin Zaha Hadid hinterlassen: Nach ihren Plänen wurde ab 2006 die neue Hungerburgbahn gebaut, die das Stadtzentrum mit „Hoch-Innsbruck" verbindet. Sie ersetzte die alte Standseilbahn, die nach 99 Jahren Betrieb eingestellt wurde – nicht nur zur Freude der Innsbrucker, von denen viele gern an der altehrwürdigen Bahn festgehalten hätten. Bereits 2001/02 hatte Zaha Hadid Innsbruck mit der neuen Bergisel-Sprungschanze sein modernes Wahrzeichen geschenkt: ein eleganter Bau, der gleichermaßen Innsbrucks Bedeutung als Sport- wie als Architekturstadt verkörpert. ■

The City in Modern Times

The ity of Innsbruck is in a constant state of change. In particular within the inner city. Numerous new buildings have emerged since the 1990s, which have resulted in an exciting and sometimes controversial connection with the historic buildings in their neighbourhood.

Innsbruck's relationship with modern architecture, however, is much older. Prior to the mid-20th century important architects such as Franz Baumann (the funicular stations of the Nordkette), Clemens Holzmeister (parish church Allerheiligen) or Lois Welzenbacher (Adambräu Brewhouse) worked in the city.

It was Lois Welzenbacher who brought Innsbruck its first skyscraper in the 1920s – the present site of Innsbruck municipal operations – and thus created an early architectural scandal. In general, modern architecture always seems to guarantee public disagreements. Such disagreements took place during Welzenbacher's time just as much as they did at the beginning of the 21st century, concerning the remodelling of the main station or the Kaufhaus Tyrol, which was rebuilt in 2010 according to plans by David Chipperfield.

The reconstruction of the Innsbruck City Hall was also accompanied by discussions regarding the possibilities and dangers of modern architecture - an elegant building, whose glass façades could symbolically represent an open, transparent city policy and where well-known artists such as Peter Kogler, Daniel Buren and Heinz Gappmayr participated in the design.

Modern architecture, however, is not limited to public buildings such as the hospital, university, museums and the new Innsbruck main station. It is also evident in housing. Over the past decades mainly the city outskirts have seen the construction of numerous new buildings, which are trying to meet the needs of its residents as well as the demands of contemporary architecture.

The most spectacular traces in the appearance of modern-day Innsbruck have probably been left by the British-Iraqi architect Zaha Hadid. In 2006 the new Hungerburgbahn funicular, connecting the city centre with "Hoch-Innsbruck" [upper Innsbruck], was built according to her design. It replaced the old funicular railway, which was discontinued after 99 years - not with everyone's blessing however, many of the inhabitants of Innsbruck would have liked to hold on to the time-honoured railway. Already in 2001/02 Zaha Hadid had presented Innsbruck with its modern landmark, the new Bergisel Ski Jump: an elegant building, which equally embodies Innsbruck's importance as a city of sports and a city of architecture. ■

Ein Röhrenlabyrinth, entworfen von Peter Kogler, überzieht den Turm im Zentrum des Rathauses.

A tube maze, designed by Peter Kogler, covers the tower in the centre of the Town Hall.

CALZEDONIA

Die Rathausgalerien sind ein Musterbeispiel für die Verbindung von moderner Architektur und Kunst: Die bunte Glasüberdachung des Hofes (links) gestaltete Daniel Buren, die Glasfassade des Turms (rechts oben) Peter Kogler, die Bronzeskulptur „Trionfante“ (rechts unten) Rudi Wach.

The Rathausgalerien are a prime example for the fusion of modern architecture and art. The colourful glass roofing of the courtyard (left) was designed by Daniel Buren, the glass façade of the tower (above right) by Peter Kogler, and the bronze sculpture "Trionfante" (bottom right) by Rudi Wach.

HISTORISCHER KONSUMTEMPEL 1908 gründeten die jüdischen Familien Bauer und Schwarz das erste Großkaufhaus in Tirol. Von Kleidung und Kosmetika bis zur Haushaltseinrichtung fand man hier alles, was das Herz begehrte – einschließlich eines Cafés für die Erholungspause vom Shopping. Im Zuge der Machtübernahme der Nationalsozialisten wurde das Kaufhaus zwangsarisiert, die Besitzer mussten emigrieren. Nach einer wechselvollen Nachkriegsgeschichte wurde der mittlerweile in „Kaufhaus Tyrol" umbenannte Konsumtempel 2010 durch einen von David Chipperfield geplanten Neubau ersetzt.

HISTORICAL TEMPLE OF CONSUMERISM *In 1908 the Jewish families Bauer and Schwarz founded the first large department store in Tyrol. From clothing and cosmetics to household furnishings, everything that your heart could desire could be found here – including a café for a break from shopping. As part of the takeover of power by the National Socialists, the department store was forcefully aryanised and the owners had to emigrate. After a turbulent post-war history, the department store, which in the meantime was called "Kaufhaus Tyrol" was replaced by a new building designed by David Chipperfield in 2010.*

Alt und neu: Vorder- (rechts) und Rückfront (unten) des Kaufhauses Tyrol kontrastieren mit den historischen Fassaden in der Nachbarschaft.

Old and new: Front (right) and rear (bottom) sections of the "Kaufhaus Tyrol", contrasting with the historic façades of the neighbourhood.

Für den Durchgang von der Maria-Theresien-Straße zum Sparkassenplatz schuf Peter Sandbichler die Lichtinstallation „47,16° Nord“.

Peter Sandbichler created the light installation “47.16 ° North” for the passage from Maria-Theresien-Straße to Sparkassenplatz.

Zeitgemäße Banken-
architektur: Das BTV-
Stadtforum (links) und
die Zentrale der Hypo
Tirol Bank (rechts).

Contemporary bank architecture: The BTV "die Bank für Tirol und Vorarlberg" [The Tyrol and Vorarlberg Bank] city forum (left) and the headquarters of Hypo Tirol Bank (right).

Die Fassade des Alten Landhauses spiegelt sich in der Glasfront des gegenüberliegenden Geschäftsgebäudes.

The façade of the old Landhaus [Seat of the Tyrolean Government] is reflected in the glass front of the office building opposite.

Das älteste Hochhaus Innsbrucks, 1926/27 von Lois Welzenbacher geplant, beherbergt die Zentrale der Innsbrucker Kommunalbetriebe.

The oldest high-rise building in Innsbruck, designed by Lois Welzenbacher in 1926/27, houses the headquarters of the municipal operations.

Zeitgleich mit dem Neubau des Innsbrucker Hauptbahnhofs 2001 bis 2004 wurde auch der benachbarte Busbahnhof neu gestaltet.

The adjacent bus station was redesigned simultaneously with the construction of Innsbruck's main station, 2001 to 2004.

Im Sudhaus der Brauerei Adambräu befindet sich heute das „aut“ als Ort der Vermittlung und Bewahrung von Architektur in Tirol.

Today the “aut”, a place of exchange and preservation of architecture in Tyrol is located in the brewhouse of the Adambräu brewery.

Im spektakulären Neubau „Headline“ der PEMA-Gruppe befinden sich unter anderem die Büroräumlichkeiten der Tiroler Tageszeitung, das Bezirksgericht und ein Hotel.

Among others the offices of, the Tiroler Tageszeitung, the district court and a hotel are located in the spectacular new building “Headline” of the PEMA Group.

Die Jesuitenkirche spiegelt sich in der Fassade des Management Center Innsbruck.

The Jesuit Church reflected in the façade of The Management Center Innsbruck.

KÄFIG MIT WILDWUCHS Kunst im öffentlichen Raum ist ein wichtiger Bestandteil moderner Stadtgestaltung – und dabei immer für öffentliche Aufregung gut, ob es sich nun um die umstrittenen Fresken Max Weilers im Innsbrucker Hauptbahnhof (1954) handelt oder um ein Kruzifix von Rudi Wach (1986), das erst mit gut 20 Jahren Verspätung auf der Innbrücke aufgestellt wurde. Für Aufregung sorgte auch Lois Weinberger mit seiner Installation „Wild Cube" am SoWi-Areal: Er errichtete eine monumentale Einfriedung aus Torstahl, die seitdem ganz dem Wirken der Natur überlassen ist. Heute wuchert in diesem „Käfig" ein üppiger Urwald inmitten der Stadt.

CAGE OF WILDERNESS *Public art is an important part of modern urban design, and always a source of public excitement as well, whether it concerns the controversial frescoes of Max Weiler in Innsbruck's main station (1954) or a Crucifix by Rudi Wach (1986), which was only erected on the Inn Bridge a good 20 years later. Lois Weinberger also caused excitement with his installation "Wild Cube" at the SoWi [Social and Economic Sciences Faculty]. He erected a monumental enclosure of reinforced steel which has since been left entirely to the workings of nature. Today a lush jungle is flourishing in this "cage" in the middle of the city.*

Auf dem Standort der ehemaligen Fennerkaserne wurde 1999 der transparente Neubau der Sozial- und Wirtschaftswissenschaftlichen Fakultät (SoWi) eröffnet.

The transparent construction of the Social and Economic Sciences Faculty (SoWi) was opened in 1999 on the site of the former Fennerkaserne [Fenner Barracks].

Der „Wild Cube“ von Lois Weinberger auf dem SoWi-Campus.

The “Wild Cube” by Lois Weinberger on the SoWi campus.

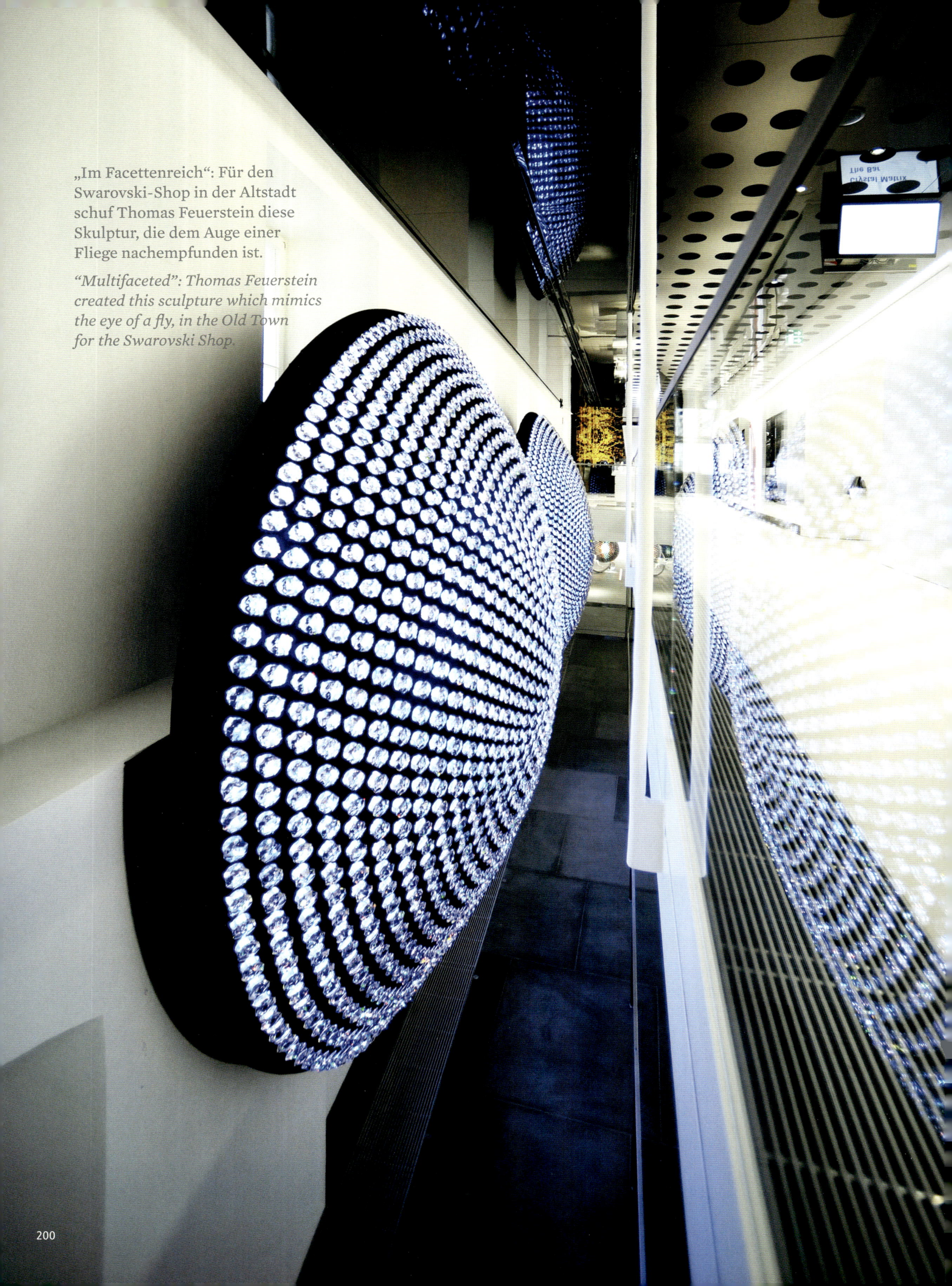

„Im Facettenreich“: Für den Swarovski-Shop in der Altstadt schuf Thomas Feuerstein diese Skulptur, die dem Auge einer Fliege nachempfunden ist.

“Multifaceted”: Thomas Feuerstein created this sculpture which mimics the eye of a fly, in the Old Town for the Swarovski Shop.

Ein Zentrum für moderne Kunst ist die Galerie im Taxispalais.

The gallery in the Taxispalais is a centre for modern art.

Auf seinen Fresken am Hauptbahnhof reflektiert Max Weiler Gegenwart und Geschichte Innsbrucks.

Max Weiler reflects on the past and present of Innsbruck in his frescoes at the main station.

Das 1973 eröffnete Kongresshaus, errichtet nach Plänen von Hubert Prachensky, ist das wichtigste Tagungszentrum der Stadt.

The Congress House opened in 1973, built according to Hubert Prachensky's design, is the main convention centre in the city.

Eine elegante Dachkonstruktion überspannt die von Zaha Hadid entworfenen Stationen der neuen Hungerburgbahn.

An elegant roof structure spans the stations of the new Hungerbahn, designed by Zaha Hadid.

In der Fassade des Restaurants „Pavillon“ am Landestheater-Vorplatz spiegelt sich die Hofburg.

The Hofburg is reflected in the façade of the restaurant "Pavillion" at the State Theatre forecourt.

Forschungseinrichtungen für Chemie, Pharmazie und Biomedizin beherbergt der neue Universitätsbau am Innrain.

The new university building on Innrain accommodates research facilities for chemistry, pharmaceuticals and biomedicine.

VOM ADERLASS ZUR HERZTRANSPLANTATION

Bereits vor über 700 Jahren erhielt Innsbruck sein erstes Krankenhaus: Knapp außerhalb der Stadtmauern wurde das Heilig-Geist-Spital am heutigen Marktgraben errichtet. Erst in den 1880er Jahren übersiedelte das Alte Spital auf ein neues Areal im Westen der Stadt. Heute kann die Innsbrucker Klinik eine beeindruckende Bilanz vorweisen, sowohl in der medizinischen Forschung als auch in der Patientenversorgung: Rund 90.000 Menschen werden pro Jahr stationär behandelt, dazu versorgt das medizinische Personal ca. eine Million Patienten ambulant und führt rund 50.000 Operationen durch.

FROM BLOOD-LETTING TO HEART TRANSPLANTS

Innsbruck had its first hospital as early as 700 years ago. Just outside the city walls, the Heilig-Geist-Spital [the Holy Spirit Hospital] was built on today's Marktgraben. The old hospital was only relocated in the 1880s to a new area in the west of the city. Today the Innsbruck clinic has an impressive record, both in medical research and in patient care. Around 90,000 people are hospitalised each year, and moreover the medical personnel treat around a million outpatients and perform approximately 50,000 surgeries.

Eines der Hauptgebäude der Klinik Innsbruck ist die 1987 eröffnete Frauen- und Kopfklinik.

One of the main buildings of the Innsbruck hospital, opened in 1987, is the Women's and Head Clinic.

Ein Zentrum des Sports in Innsbruck: die Olympiaworld mit dem Tivoli-Fußballstadion (unten) mit angeschlossener Kletterhalle und zwei Eishallen (oben).

A centre of sport in Innsbruck, the Olympiaworld with the Tivoli Football Stadium (bottom) and it's attached indoor climbing wall and two ice rinks (above).

Dreimal – 1964, 1976 und bei den Jugend-Winterspielen 2012 – brannte das Olympische Feuer im Stadion der Bergisel-Sprungschanze.

Three times, 1964, 1976 and at the Winter Youth Games in 2012, the Olympic flame has burned in the Bergisel Ski Jump Stadium.

ES LEBE DER SPORT Innsbruck ist nicht nur ein Zentrum des Breiten-, sondern auch eines des Spitzensports, und das seit vielen Jahrzehnten: 1927 fand am Bergisel der erste Skisprungbewerb statt, dessen Sieger bei exakt 47,5 Metern landete, und 1935 gab es die ersten Bob-Weltmeisterschaften in Igls – noch auf einer Naturbahn. Viele Sportstätten entstanden im Rahmen der Olympischen Winterspiele von 1964 und 1976, wurden jedoch laufend modernisiert: etwa die neue Bergisel-Schanze, eines der modernen Wahrzeichen der Stadt, oder die zwei Eishallen in der Olympiaworld, in denen neben Sportveranstaltungen auch Konzerte und Großevents stattfinden.

LONG LIVE SPORT *Innsbruck is not only a centre for recreational sports, but also one of the top centres for professional sporting events and has been for many decades. In 1927 the first ski jumping competition took place at Bergisel, the winner landed at exactly 47.5 metres and in 1935 the first bob sled world championships took place in Igls – still on a natural track. Many sports facilities were created as part of the Winter Olympic Games of 1964 and 1976 but have been constantly modernised: such as the new Bergisel jump, one of the modern landmarks of the city, and the two ice rinks in the Olympiaworld, in which concerts and large events take place in addition to sporting events.*

Zur 50. Vierschanzentournee 2002 wurde die nach Plänen von Zaha Hadid neu errichtete Bergisel-Schanze eingeweiht.

In 2002, for the 50th Vierschanzentournee [Four Hills Tournament] the newly built Bergisel ski jump, designed by Zaha Hadid, was inaugurated.

Vielfältige Stadtränder

Die Randbezirke von Innsbruck sind ein Raum der Gegensätze: Moderne Wohnsiedlungen verweisen auf das Wachstum einer Stadt, deren Bevölkerungszahl sich seit 1900 mehr als verdoppelt hat. Ausgedehnte Gewerbegebiete mit großen Einkaufszentren zeugen vom wirtschaftlichen Gewicht der Landeshauptstadt, die innerhalb Tirols eine dominierende Stellung einnimmt.

Zugleich begegnet man an den Rändern auch einem ganz anderen Gesicht von Innsbruck: Stadtteile wie Hötting, Mühlau und Arzl an den Hängen der Nordkette oder, auf der gegenüberliegenden Talseite, Pradl, Amras, Vill und Igls haben bis heute einen Teil ihres dörflichen Charakters bewahrt – nicht nur im Erscheinungsbild der alten Dorfkerne, sondern auch im Bewusstsein der alteingesessenen Bewohner, die deren Identität und Traditionen unter anderem in zahlreichen Vereinen pflegen.

Hervorgegangen sind diese Stadtteile aus Dörfern und Fraktionen, die sich über Jahrhunderte hinweg eigenständig entwickelt haben und erst im Verlauf des 20. Jahrhunderts – insbesondere während der Zeit des Nationalsozialismus – eingemeindet wurden. So war Hötting früher nicht nur ein wohlhabendes Bauerndorf, sondern auch ein Zentrum des Bergbaus: Wandert man von Hötting aus bergwärts, stößt man immer noch auf Knappenlöcher, aus denen bis vor 250 Jahren Silber und Kupfer abgebaut wurde.

Mühlau dagegen war bereits sehr früh ein Industriezentrum: Schon im Mittelalter wurden in Plattnerwerkstätten Harnische angefertigt, am Mühlauer Bach wurden Sägewerke und Mühlen betrieben. Igls, im Mittelgebirge 300 Meter über dem Talboden gelegen, wandelte sich im 19. Jahrhundert vom kleinen Bauerndorf zur beliebten Sommerfrische – nah an der Stadt, mit einer Mittelgebirgs-Straßenbahn rasch zu erreichen, und dennoch in der Natur. Seit den Olympischen Winterspielen 1964 und 1976, deren Bewerbe zum Teil dort ausgetragen wurden, ist Igls darüber hinaus auch ein Zentrum des internationalen Wintersports.

Auf eine ganz andere Art hat Olympia seine Spuren am östlichen Rand von Innsbruck hinterlassen: Aus den Olympischen Dörfern der Winterspiele von 1964 und 1976 ging ein Stadtteil hervor, der heute knapp 7.000 Menschen beherbergt – damit zählt das Olympische Dorf gemeinsam mit der benachbarten Reichenau zu den am dichtesten besiedelten Stadtteilen.

Und auch am westlichen Stadtrand wuchsen neue Wohngebiete, die Raum für die stetig wachsende Stadtbevölkerung schufen. Große Wohnanlagen wie zum Beispiel die Peerhofsiedlung entstanden dort, aber auch die unverwechselbaren Siedlungen am Lohbach und im Sieglanger: In den 1930er Jahren wurden hier kleine Reihen- und Einfamilienhäuser inmitten von viel Grün errichtet, die seither Teil der vielfältigen Stadtränder Innsbrucks sind. ■

The Diversity of the Outskirts

The outskirts of Innsbruck form an area of contrasts: modern housing developments indicate the growth of a city whose population has more than doubled since 1900. Extensive commercial areas with major shopping centres are evidence of the economic importance of the state capital, which occupies a dominant position within Tyrol.

At the same time one encounters a very different aspect of Innsbruck in the outskirts. Districts such as Hötting, Mühlau and Arzl on the slopes of the Nordkette or, on the opposite side of the valley, Pradl, Amras, Vill and Igls have preserved a part of their rural character to this day. Not only in the appearance of the old village centres, but also in the consciousness of the long-established residents, who have maintained their identity and traditions, also in numerous societies and clubs.

These city districts arose from villages and factions, which developed independently over the centuries and were only incorporated during the course of the 20th century – in particular during the time of National Socialism. Hötting was not only a prosperous farming village, but also a centre for mining. If you walk from Hötting up the mountain, you can still encounter mining holes from which silver and copper were mined up to 250 years ago.

Mühlau, on other hand, was an industrial centre very early on. In the Middle Ages armour was already being made in workshops and sawmills and mills were being operated on the Mühlauer Bach [Mühlauer stream]. Igls, located 300 meters above the valley floor in the Mittelgebirge [a low mountain range], was transformed in the 19th century from a small farming village into a popular summer resort close to the city, which was easily accessible by tramway and yet in the midst of nature. Since the Winter Olympics in 1964 and 1976, during which some sporting competitions were held in Igls, the district has additionally become an international centre for winter sports.

The Olympic Games left a completely different mark on the eastern outskirts of Innsbruck. The Olympic Villages of the Winter Games of 1964 and 1976 developed into a district, which is home to almost 7,000 people today. The Olympic Village, together with the adjacent Reichenau, has consequently become one of the most densely populated districts.

New residential areas have also sprung up on the western outskirts, creating space for the growing urban population. Large residential complexes, such as the Peerhofsiedlung, have been created there, as well as the distinctive settlements in Lohbach and Sieglanger. In the 1930s, small terraced houses and single-family homes were built in the middle of greenery, and have since become part of the diverse city outskirts of Innsbruck. ■

Im Osten von Innsbruck liegen zwei seiner größten Wohnsiedlungen: Die Reichenau (rechts) und das Olympische Dorf (links), das aus den Athletenwohnheimen der Olympischen Spiele entstanden ist.

In the east of Innsbruck are two of its biggest housing estates: The Reichenau (right) and the Olympic Village (left), which sprung from the athletes' accommodation built for the Olympic Games.

Neue Wohnungen wurden in den vergangenen Jahren auch in der Bienerstraße im Stadtteil Saggen geschaffen.

New apartments have also been built in recent years on Bienerstraße in Saggen.

SIEDLERGEIST Auf dem sumpfigen Boden der Ulfiswiese am Lohbach entstand in den 1930er Jahren ein neuer Stadtteil: kleine Siedlungshäuser, die mit viel persönlichem Arbeitseinsatz erbaut wurden, und in deren Gärten Obstbäume gepflanzt, Gemüsebeete und kleine Äcker angelegt wurden – so konnten sich die Bewohner in den harten Zwischenkriegsjahren wenigstens zum Teil selbst versorgen. Bis heute hat die Lohbachsiedlung ihren ursprünglichen Charakter bewahrt. Und bis heute lebendig ist auch der Gemeinschaftsgeist der Bewohner, die sich zum Siedlerverein „Am Lohbach“ zusammengeschlossen haben.

SETTLER SPIRIT *In the 1930s a new district emerged on the marshy ground of the Ulfis meadowland along the Lohbach. Small settlement houses were built using a lot of personal labour, where fruit trees and vegetables were planted in gardens, and small fields were created. Therefore the residents were at least partly self-sufficient in the hard interwar years. To date, the Lohbachsiedlung has retained its original character. And to this day the community spirit of the residents, who have come together in a settlers' society named "Am Lohbach", has remained lively.*

Wohnräume am westlichen Stadtrand: die Lohbachsiedlung und die Peerhofsiedlung in Hötting West.

Living space on the western outskirts: the Lohbachsiedlung and Peerhofsiedlung in Hötting West.

Seit der Gründung der Stadt ist Innsbruck ein Verkehrsknotenpunkt – heute führt eine der wichtigsten Transitrouten zwischen Nord- und Südeuropa an der Stadt vorbei.

Since the founding of the city, Innsbruck has been a transport hub. Today one of the most important transit routes between northern and southern Europe run past the city.

Wohnen im Grünen: Der Stadtteil Hötting West reicht bis zu den Auen des Lohbachs.

Living in the countryside: Hötting West extends up to the floodplains of the Lohbach.

Auf eine wechselvolle Geschichte blickt Schloss Mentlberg zurück, das unter anderem Kaserne, Hotel und Lazarett war.

Mentlberg castle looks back on an eventful history, having been a barracks, a hotel and a hospital.

Unter dem Park von Schloss Mentlberg breiten sich die westlichen Stadtteile von Innsbruck aus.

The western districts of the city of Innsbruck spread out under the park of Mentlberg Castle.

STÄDTISCHE LANDWIRTSCHAFT Mehrere Stadtteile an den Rändern Innsbrucks sind aus eigenständigen Dörfern hervorgegangen, bevor sie im Lauf des 20. Jahrhunderts eingemeindet wurden. Auch wenn sich der Charakter dieser Stadtteile – nicht zuletzt durch den starken Zuzug – verändert hat, ist die dörfliche Identität in Mühlau und Arzl, Vill und Igls, Hötting oder auch in Teilen von Amras und Pradl nach wie vor spürbar. Hier findet man auch heute noch Bauernhöfe mitten im Stadtgebiet: Mehr als 150 landwirtschaftliche Betriebe gibt es in Innsbruck, auf denen über 4.000 Stück Vieh leben – manche von ihnen dürfen die Sommer auf den bewirtschafteten Almen an der Nordkette und am Patscherkofel verbringen.

URBAN AGRICULTURE *Many districts at the outskirts of Innsbruck were independent villages before they were incorporated during the 20th century. Even if the character of these neighbourhoods – not least on account of the strong influx of people – has changed, the village identity in Mühlau and Arzl, Vill and Igls, Hötting, and also in parts of Amras and Pradl, is still noticeable. Here you can still find farms in the middle of urban areas, even today. More than 150 farms are still in business in Innsbruck, supporting around 4,000 head of cattle – some of which are allowed to spend their summer on the mountain pastures of the Nordkette and on Patscherkofel.*

Im Mittelpunkt des alten Dorfkerns von Pradl steht der Brunnen mit der Figur des heiligen Florian.

At the centre of the old village of Pradl is a fountain with the statue of St. Florian.

Vill hat seinen dörflichen Charakter
bis in die Gegenwart bewahrt.

*Vill has retained its rural character
to the present day.*

Am Übergang zwischen Stadt und Natur:
Arzl im Osten von Innsbruck.

At the transition between city and nature:
Arzl in the east of Innsbruck.

Franz Andreas Sternbach, der als Bergwerksbesitzer zu Reichtum gekommen war, ließ sich im 18. Jahrhundert in Mühlau das „Sternbachschlössl“ errichten, zu dem auch eine Schlosskapelle gehört.

In the 18th century, Franz Andreas Sternbach, who came to wealth as a mine owner, built the “Sternbachschlössl”, which also included a chapel, in Mühlau.

1539 ließ der Geschützgießer Gregor Löffler den Ansitz Büchsenhausen in St. Nikolaus erbauen.

In 1539 the cannon and bell founder Gregor Löffler built Büchsenhausen in St. Nikolaus.

Die Weiherburg neben dem Alpenzoo trägt ihren Namen nach einem Fischweiher, an dessen Ufer sie im 15. Jahrhundert entstand.

The Weiherburg next to the Alpine Zoo is named after a fish pond, upon whose banks it was built in the 15th century.

GONDELFAHRT AUF DER HUNGERBURG Kurz nach der Jahrhundertwende war die Hungerburg ein beliebtes Naherholungsgebiet. 1912 wurde dort ein einzigartiger Freizeitpark eröffnet: ein großer künstlicher Badesee mit Wasserfall, Liegeterrassen und Ruderbooten, und ein Aussichtsturm, der an die Ruine einer mittelalterlichen Burg erinnerte, aber mit einem hochmodernen Lift erreicht werden konnte – um 20 Heller (inklusive Gondelfahrt). In den 1920er Jahren wurde dem See das Wasser abgedreht und der Freizeitpark geschlossen. Auf seinem Gelände befindet sich heute das Bildungshaus Seehof der Tiroler Arbeiterkammer.

CABLE CAR RIDE ON THE HUNGERBURG *At the turn of the century the Hungerburg was a popular local recreational area. In 1912 a unique amusement park was opened. It had: a large artificial lake with a waterfall, sun deck and rowing boats, and an observation tower, reminiscent of the ruins of a medieval castle, but could be reached using a highly modern lift for 20 Heller (including gondola ride). In the 1920s, the water to the lake was turned off and the amusement park was closed. Today the Seehof Educational Centre for the Tyrolean Labour Union is located on its premises.*

Bereits vor 100 Jahren wurden die Ausflügler im Gasthaus zur Linde verköstigt – mittlerweile befindet sich darin ein Kindergarten.

Already a hundred years ago, tourists were entertained in the Guest House zur Linde – now home to a children's nursery.

Nur noch der Aussichtsturm erinnert heute an den ehemaligen Freizeitpark auf der Hungerburg.

Now it is only the lookout tower that reminds one of the former amusement park on Hungerburg.